THE REST OF ME

RICHARD PATTERSON

THE REST OF ME

iUniverse books may be ordered through booksellers or by contacting:

iUniverse
1663 Liberty Drive
Bloomington, IN 47403
www.iuniverse.com
844-349-9409

Because of the dynamic nature of the Internet, any web addresses or links contained in this book may have changed since publication and may no longer be valid. The views expressed in this work are solely those of the author and do not necessarily reflect the views of the publisher, and the publisher hereby disclaims any responsibility for them.

Any people depicted in stock imagery provided by Getty Images are models, and such images are being used for illustrative purposes only. Certain stock imagery © Getty Images.

ISBN: 978-1-6632-2650-1 (sc)
ISBN: 978-1-6632-2649-5 (e)

Library of Congress Control Number: 2022909210

Print information available on the last page.

iUniverse rev. date: 06/06/2022

A legacy for my children and grandchildren.
A life unsung is a life unknown.

To my wonderful wife, Janie, for her undying encouragement.

CONTENTS

PREFACE

In the last quarter of my life, a thought came to me: *Should I write a story about my life as a historical legacy for those interested?* Of course, these remembrances are cobbled together and often propelled by a faulty memory. In spite of this, I believe this book tells a true story of family, friends, and me. Everyone has a story, but few are able or willing to tell it. Every life is fascinating, filled with wonderment and awe. This world is less as people's stories follow them to the grave untold.

Historically, oral tellings were the norm. This is still a powerful medium; however, at some point, a story must be written down, or it will be lost forever. This story is not spectacular but, I believe, quite ordinary. By the very act of my writing it, it becomes extraordinary. The people in the story who are long past come to life with the telling of this tale. A sense of immortality descends upon the written word. Others may be able to tell it better, but I dared get into the arena.

CHAPTER 1

―⁓ɯ⁓―

Preparative Words

The beginning seems a reasonable place to start; however, in the telling of this story, I must go beyond beginnings to the nascent narrative concerning my parents, Bill and Irene. This preamble sets the stage for an interesting story. A brief recounting of family lineage helps to launch the ensuing chronicle.

My mother, Irene, endured and overcame an incredible hardscrabble existence. She was the fourth oldest of four sisters and one brother. They were hillbillies in Oklahoma. Their "betters" in the community knew them as "white trash." Desperately poor, they were in fact "poor white trash." Irene lived in a sod dugout home on the Oklahoma prairie—in effect, a hole in the ground overlaid with sod. She had a lifelong fear and prejudice against American Indians, birthed as a little girl upon seeing Indians silhouetted against the horizon. This was obviously an irrational fear, but it was real for this little girl. Each night before bed, her mother, Mae—a nervous, small, hunchbacked woman—would gather the children and venture out of the dugout to hunt and kill the ubiquitous rattlesnakes, making it safer for all to sleep at night.

Irene's father abandoned the family early, but the cumberground would periodically visit just long enough to impregnate Mae. On one of these visits, he sexually violated little Irene. This was a hard start for a little girl. There was no benefit of psychotherapy or mentoring involved in helping her overcome the trauma. Her entire upbringing was rather horrid. As she grew, she became a beautiful young lady like those pictured in fairy tales, except this story is real and not fictional.

Irene was sent to live with her older sister Maggie, who was truly a wicked woman. She had accumulated much wealth by sundry nefarious means. This woman would swindle people out of real estate, oil wells, and more, lying and cheating herself to wealth. Along the way, it was rumored she had killed two of her husbands. This sister could well have been a psychopath. She reportedly was run out of town on suspicion of setting a house fire that resulted in the death of a small girl. There also were strong indications she had pushed a little playmate from a bridge to her death. She constantly tried to poison Irene. Even as a grown woman, Irene fell ill if ever she ate food prepared by Maggie. This evil older sister often engaged in an incestuous relationship with her father, claiming he was the best lover she had ever experienced. It was also strongly believed she euthanized her saintly uncle and her own mother, Mae.

Maggie eventually married Paul, a gay chiropractor. He claimed to be quite an organist; however, he was never heard to play the instrument. When visiting Irene and Maggie, he was always looking to give so-called adjustments, especially to the children. Irene never allowed the kids to be alone with Paul, an effeminate man with a pencil-thin mustache who claimed that in the war, he'd had the misfortune of having his testicles shot off by an enemy soldier. It could have been true but probably was not. Irene was on high alert if ever a sexual predator was about. The few times Paul and Maggie came for a visit to California to see the family, they would drive their pink Cadillac convertible with white leather interior, in effect flaunting their wealth to their poorer relations.

Maggie had a profitable business providing abortions and operating a house of prostitution. In that toxic milieu, Irene, as a young girl, was tasked with working under threat of deprivations and beatings. Her jobs included doing maid service, cleaning after abortions, and entertaining the men by sitting on their laps. Having no choice, she was forced to work in that hellish environment, but she overcame all that was placed before her and, in the process, developed nerves of steel and an iron will. She did not have the luxury of a calm, safe childhood.

How ironic life can be. In Maggie's last month of life, as she lay on her deathbed, surrounded by her wealth, her sister Irene, whom she had so maligned, attended to her. Irene was a kind, forgiving person. While visiting Maggie in her last days, she found it astonishing to see how much wealth and money were strewn about the house. Of course, the fortune was like honey to flies, attracting various extended family members who arrived to scoop up the largesse along with entire rooms of furniture. Greed is a great revealer of people's character.

This is a brief overview of Irene's early years. Now I will introduce William Oliver, my dad.

William had an unbelievably difficult beginning by any measure. He grew up in Arkansas and Oklahoma and became completely independent by age eleven after losing his mother and father. His mother died from cancer when he was just a little boy, so he never knew much about her. His father was a nonfunctional alcoholic who eventually died in the gutter on some street in Los Angeles. No family member wanted to take on the responsibility of caring for the little boy—a black mark upon this family. Bill, known to his friends as Red because of his ginger hair, wandered the streets and byways and rode boxcars on the rails as he traveled the country.

At age eleven, while kicking a can down the street in the small town of Heavener, Oklahoma, he met another little boy his age. They struck up a friendship, as little boys often do, and the boy invited Bill to come have lunch at his home. This was rather propitious, as the boy's father was the town judge. The judge and his son were living with the judge's sister at her home. This lady, known as Aunt Fern, allowed Bill to live with them. This afforded young Bill a respite and a quasifamily for a few years.

However, it was not a healthy environment, as Fern was an old-maid lesbian living with her mean partner, Kathleen. Leaving Heavener, Bill moved on and became a hobo, working as an itinerant crop picker. His mode of transportation was the railroads. As he grew, he worked for the Civilian Conservation Corps during the Great Depression. He later worked as a lumberjack in California, harvesting ponderosa pines and redwood trees. At one time, he even worked on the iconic Golden Gate Bridge.

Bill only finished the sixth grade but was an intelligent man. Well read and self-taught, he was able to do about anything using his hands, such as building a home without any help or benefit of power tools. Bill, a voracious reader, testified to French philosopher Albert Camus's contention that most education is obtained not from university professors but from one's own library of books.

Irene and Bill met at a dance and quickly married after he raised enough money by selling some chickens and three cows. Irene's dysfunctional family never liked Bill, believing Irene could have done better. However, three of her sisters and her brother Ross liked him. Bill and Irene married, and together with Aunt Pearl and her philandering husband, Preston, they traveled to California, taking about two weeks to make the journey in a Model T Ford. Playing and singing in honky-tonks and staying in the local YMCAs on the way, they made it to the promised land of opportunity, a.k.a. Los Angeles, with eleven cents in their pockets.

Bill quickly got a job trimming palm trees, for which he was never paid. He was fortunate in getting employment at a petrol oil refinery, where he remained for forty-five years as it underwent ownership changes from Douglas Oil to Conoco Oil. This enabled him to provide for a family and live in a house built by his own hands.

This preamble now gets us to the beginning of this story.

CHAPTER 2

Faintest of Remembrances

Richard was born in 1945, about two years after his sister Shirley and two years before his sister Sue. Maywood Hospital was his birthplace, and a brown house was his first home. Of course, there is little remembrance of the early years, but there are fond memories of Shirley, his beautiful auburn-haired big sister. She introduced him to the joy of eating fresh dandelions and sucking the sweet nectar from honeysuckle stems. She also taught him patience in locating four-leafed clovers, a momentous find back in the day. They laughed often as they went about their days attending to important matters.

The family had a small home, the aforementioned brown house, with the smallest of kitchens. There was an icebox, not a refrigerator, which the ice man replenished about every five days. A simple ice pick was used for chipping off small pieces of ice to make iced tea. Richard, however, out of an early scientific sense of curiosity, used the pick one day to puncture a milk carton, and he was amazed at the resultant little milkfall cascading to the floor. No discipline ensued from this untoward adventure. However, little grace was extended concerning his next curious endeavor: his attempt to paint his father's black car white. His antics, now not so cute, earned him a swat to his porcelain bottom.

Two blocks from the home were railroad tracks. Trains fascinated Richard. When his mother would take him for a walk, they would often cross the tracks, on which he wanted to play. After placing rocks or other objects on the rails, he would excitedly wait to see what happened as a train passed. This exasperated his mother, as she envisioned her son escaping her grasp and being crushed on the tracks like the rocks. Unfortunately, a man did fall onto the rails once, resulting in the amputation of both legs and his demise. Mom apparently thought there might be a lesson for the kids concerning the terrible event, as she took them to view the ghastly sight. Richard still remembers the scene seventy-five years later. Parents can be interesting and, retrospectively, odd.

But this is not the end of the train stories. Later, there will be a recounting of the real life-and-death challenge of a prepubescent boy of ten in the wilds of New Mexico.

Overall, the memories of living in the brown house are pleasant. The unfolding of Richard's life from childhood to young adulthood, as outlined in the next chapter, occurred in Norwalk, California.

CHAPTER 3

Early Childhood

Richard's parents purchased two large lots in a sparsely settled neighborhood that would eventually be populated by row upon row of single-story, flat-topped stucco houses. This became known as the flat-top district and soon morphed into a Mexican barrio. Due to his low self-esteem, living in a barrio caused Richard much embarrassment as a teenager.

His first remembrance is of living in a small trailer on Hayford Street and bathing in a large metal tub prominently displayed in the yard. Modesty was an early imprint on his id, so bathing in that fashion was mortifying to him. Being naked for all the world to view was an early trauma akin to seeing a dead man lying next to railroad tracks. A four-year-old hillbilly bathing in an outdoor tub seemed about right for this family.

His father, employed at Douglas Oil, would come home after work and continue construction on the twelve-hundred-square-foot house. This marvel of construction consisted of one bathroom (indoors), two bedrooms, a kitchen, a living room, and a dining room. He worked tirelessly, doing all the work by himself with just occasional help from Uncle Bill.

Uncle Bill was married to Aunt Pearl, or Auntie, as she was affectionately known. She had long ago jettisoned philandering Preston. As far as storytellers went, few rivaled Uncle Bill, with the possible exception of Uncle Omar. Every word was masterfully embellished, and any boy would have loved to be around him, with his never-ending cascade of stories. However, no one Richard knew could top the outlandish storytelling of Uncle Omar. His story of a black panther matching his every step as he walked through the woods at dusk just off the trail to his right, weaving in and out of the shadows, was thrilling. He would take his time, speaking slowly, all the while with a twinkle in his eye. Whether he was spinning a tale about a monster mule or a charging alligator, there was a ring of truth somewhere in the story. When he began unleashing a mighty stem-winder with or without the encouragement of alcohol, the kids knew everything coming out of his mouth was probably untrue, but it didn't matter; they hung on his every word. Something inside said, *You know, this could be true.* He was tall and lanky, speaking with a drawl, and endearingly, he obviously did not take himself too seriously. He would spin tales concerning every subject, with some being birthed out of thin air. After rolling his own cigarettes and pouring himself a shot of cheap whiskey, he would serenade all with honky-tonk music on his tinny-sounding piano as he puffed on a drooping cigarette while smiling. There was something genuine about Omar that Richard liked, and he enjoyed being around that bona fide hillbilly.

Richard's dad performed all the work on the family house, from foundation to finish-out. He used only hand tools, and it took him about a year to complete the task. During this time, little sister Sue was about eighteen months old. This freckle-faced, redheaded little girl was active and hard to keep up with. She once ascended halfway up a ladder to the roof, where Dad was working. With amazement, Richard gazed upon his fearless little sister hauling herself and her heavy-hanging soiled diaper up the ladder, teetering on the brink of disaster. Thanks be to God for Sue's sake that Mother came running out of the trailer, yelling at poor Dad, who was able to snatch Sue from certain ruin.

Early childhood on Hayford Street settled into a comfortable, safe blur. Day to day, growing in a cocoon of parental and sibling love with acceptance was the rhythm. The family was still tethered to its white, somewhat poor roots. There was a subtle pushback by Richard against this perceived shame.

The neighborhood was sparsely settled, so there were few kids to play with. Playing with one another was the entertainment of the day. At an early age, it was clear Richard had an anger problem manifesting in a quick temper. Teasing was easily served but difficult to eat. The response to a perceived insult was immediate physical retaliation, usually in the form of hitting or choking. This anger often manifested in his chasing his sisters through fields of sunflowers, trying unsuccessfully to choke the life out of them.

In the house one day, while he was holding court and spewing a torrent of acerbic taunts directed toward his favorite prey, his sisters, Shirley, the oldest, had the temerity to send back a rejoinder addressing one of his taunts. Immediately, he straddled her, employing his patented choke hold, trying his best to send her prematurely into the afterlife. At that point, dear Mother intervened and began a primitive three-step program to help control this rage monster, which, if left unchecked, portended a poor future. Still, there are vestiges of rage at seventy-five years of age, which especially manifest on highways populated by morons.

Overall, the boy had a pleasant childhood filled with familiar, comfortable routines. Grayland Avenue Elementary School was his introduction to public education. Recollections of the five years spent there are affable except for two episodes: soiling himself and having a life-and-death experience. In the former incident, upon leaving school one day and beginning the six-block journey home, Richard had an overwhelming urge to evacuate his bowels. Being six years old and somewhat confused about the impending event, he began dropping little, hard, condensed rabbit-like pellets down inside his pants. They accumulated near his shoes. Pure mortification gripped him as the accident unfolded. Glancing quickly, ensuring no one had witnessed the spectacle, the perpetrator moved adroitly away from the accusing pellets. After making it home in record time, he cleansed himself without ever being found out. Slowly, he started honing his skill set in the art of leading a double life.

The second memorable event that occurred, bordering on life and death, was contracting scarlet fever in the third grade. Not feeling well, he was sent to the school nurse. Realizing the boy was really sick, she drove the delirious boy home. He does not remember arriving. The golden-haired child did not regain consciousness for two weeks. The house was put under quarantine for the duration, restricting Mother and both sisters to a form of house arrest. Dad was allowed to go to work, but after work, he had to return immediately home again. The family physician, old Dr. Hoffman, who'd been raised and trained in Germany, nursed the ill student back to health. This old gentleman made daily house calls, though Richard was unaware of any but the last few. Being absent from conscious life for about two weeks had a sobering effect on Richard. A nascent sense of mortality came into view for the first time.

After a while, things returned to normal, except Richard was left in a weakened condition. Mother started plying the boy with cod liver oil, Carter's Little Liver Pills, and sundry home remedies, including hot toddies; Vicks VapoRub in the nose and slathered on his sunken chest, overlaid with warm compresses; occasional laxatives; blackstrap molasses; and various aromatic hard candies, all designed to ward off the so-called failure-to-thrive syndrome, rheumatic fever, dreaded polio, and the development of flat feet. Richard seamlessly morphed back into the golden child. Of course, his sisters pushed back against this coronation and to this day do not recognize this title.

He was pretty much a homebody in the early years. He enjoyed playing with electric trains, riding his bicycle, and playing cowboys and Indians or cops and robbers. The fun was immensely enhanced if cap guns were employed. Summers, which lasted three months, seemed to be endless, carefree times with little to worry about.

CHAPTER 4

Polio and Such

Everyone was aware of polio and the attendant dreaded iron lung, a grotesque contraption that breathed for the paralyzed person. Swimming in public pools was frowned upon during polio outbreaks, some of which lasted most of the summer. Richard, however, seldom went to the pool, since he did not know how to swim, so it was really no problem for him. During these polio epidemics, the best defense was to stay away from large groups of people and use common sense, which seemed to be in ample supply in those days. As an aside, consider how poorly the COVID-19 pandemic has been handled in 2020. First off, who eats bat soup, pangolin patties, monkey brains, rhino horns, or tiger treats? What is a wet market but a veritable petri dish of pathogens? Because of the mishandling of this pandemic (scamdemic), the experts demand all people stay home, stop working, don't associate, and wear masks. Sick people need to be quarantined, not healthy people. This has never been done before on this scale and flies in the face of basic epidemiology. More sinister reasons probably lie behind these decisions.

The consequences of a broken economy with no jobs is catastrophic. More people will die from other causes than from COVID-19. Richard survived polio epidemics, multiple hot wars, and a long cold war, with its attendant Cuban Missile Crisis and narrowly avoided nuclear holocaust. He also survived the horrible flu season of 1986–87, SARS, MERS, Ebola, and others. Life went on, but not with this engineered Chinese flu. How easily common sense is extinguished.

About that time, a wonderful doctor, Jonas Salk, developed a prevention for polio, but it could only be administered by a dreaded needle injection into one's arm. Waxing and waning over the ponderous question of whether it would be better to get polio or receive the painful injection, Richard kept coming down on the side of getting polio.

The school year commenced, and Richard began third grade. When the second week was about over, Richard found himself in a slow-moving line with moaning sounds emanating from the front. In answer to his fevered questions, his hapless classmates informed him they were in line to receive the dreaded polio needle. About to swoon, Richard suddenly found himself at the head of the moaning line. Quickly calculating his response and possible escape route, he felt a strong hand grip his skinny arm. He opened his squinted eyes just in time to see what appeared to be a dull and blunted six-foot-long needle taking dead aim at his pathetic arm. Being rather nimble-witted, Richard thought now might be a good time to tighten up and flex his small-boy bicep, hoping it might deflect the needle. He realized too late this was a poor decision, as the needle pierced his muscular defenses, depositing the Salk vaccine into a now withered arm. He didn't pass out but was dancing around the edges of consciousness.

What a dastardly trick the public health officials played upon their innocent young charges. Oh, how the cosmos was against little Richard that day when he learned this ritual would be repeated in about two weeks. At this point, the boy was quite willing to end his education at the third grade. Somehow, and only the Muses know how, he staggered through the second inoculation and then learned the third dose would be delivered on the wings of a dove in the form of a sugar cube. This was probably the beginning of his spiritual journey.

His nascent religious stirrings had a certain velleity about them, certainly not at the Damascus Road level. His beloved older sister Shirley seemed to always have an intimate relationship with Jesus; some believed she had come out of the womb praising Him. This was not the case with the rest of the household.

Mother and Father, not being particularly spiritual, realized there would be an eternal cost to pay for the dereliction of their spiritual duties, so they abrogated their responsibilities and encouraged Mr. and Mrs. Cummings, who lived three houses away, to transport the three kids to church most Sundays. The farming out of these duties to various people and churches resulted in Richard coming to a saving faith and being baptized at age twelve. Attending a Billy Graham revival meeting in Los Angeles with his mom, his sisters, Aunt Easter, and her three daughters made a powerful impression on Richard as he witnessed hundreds of people in various states of excitement and agitation being convicted of their sins. As the invitation was given to come forward, Richard did not obey, but he had a strong sense something was not right in his soul. *Cumberground* was not a word in his vocabulary, but it fit him perfectly.

When he attended a Pentecostal church one Sunday soon after the revival, the Holy Spirit allowed him to see himself as he was. Not liking what he saw, he went forward to confess his brokenness and accept the gracious offer of salvation offered by Jesus. The burden of sin and shame was immediately lifted from his shoulders and placed on the scarred back of Christ. However, having no spiritual mentors or real church home and without any encouragement to read the scriptures, he was a sitting duck for Satan's schemes. He quickly reverted to his comfortable carnality. The slow, painful work of sanctification is where the real story lies, and the remainder of this narrative will reveal this.

CHAPTER 5

—◠◠—

Death Spectra

A number of events occurred between ages ten and twelve. Richard's uncle Ross, who always smiled and was talkative, had four sons, and they lived in New Mexico. Richard, with family, traveled there one summer for vacation. In the span of only one week, Richard experienced four near-death episodes, which might be a record for a ten-year-old boy. Some might quibble with the first one, which involved his introduction to New Mexico cuisine.

As he was a tender ten-year-old who had never tasted tacos, tamales, or tostadas, Richard's taste buds were tattered at the initial tasting. He cried out in torment as his mouth was torched; the pain was unrelenting. The vicinal population of Latinos were grieved as they realized they inadvertently had damaged this golden-haired child with torchy tacos. No amount of water, milk, or praying had any soothing effect on taming the torture as the child began speaking in tongues. However, time always heals, and the pain gradually subsided. Years later, he eventually acquired a taste for tacos *sans serranos*.

The next day morphed into an unusual day as he was introduced to the neighborhood swimming pool. This pool was nothing more than a large, deep hole that had been bulldozed into the ground. Richard could not swim and had a great fear of water. This did not dissuade his father one bit, hence the ensuing fiasco.

His dad, trying to solve both problems, his fear and his inability to swim, in one brilliant move, decided to toss Richard into the deep end of the pool in view of all the kids. Unlike the apostle Peter of the Bible, Richard was unable to walk on the water, but he gave it his best effort. Instead, he found himself treading at the bottom of the hole. Each time he surfaced to inhale a fresh breath of glorious air, he went straight to the bottom again. As with Paul the apostle, there were moments, maybe two or three, spent going in and out of the third heaven.

Finally, as he clawed himself to the edge of the wretched hole, his voice was restored. What had been a pleasant little-boy contralto now was a high-C tenor in the style of Luciano Pavarotti. This unusual vocalization brought the pool festivities to a sudden halt and blessed Mother to her feet. Father, severely chastised, was forced to jump into the water to rescue his sissy son. Obviously, the man had no future as a swimming coach, and his son had none as an accomplished swimmer. However, later in Richard's life, there would be a scuba experience.

The following day, trying to forget the torchy tacos and his singing debut at the pool, Richard, with three cousins, decided to go exploring. Venturing along a dry riverbed, they happened to find themselves in quicksand. Watching westerns on television had convinced them of their impending doom. Richard was up to his knees and sinking fast. His cousins, not wanting a dead cousin on their résumés, started offering Richard sticks and other life-saving devices, and they gradually pulled him from the Machiavellian mud. This, his third near-death experience in a mere three days, mandated a rest period.

Sitting on dry ground, recounting all the intricacies of this most amazing rescue in great, embellished detail, they screwed up their courage to go home and explain Richard's befouled appearance. Being sages at ten and twelve years of age, they decided to take a shortcut, walking an eighth of a mile on a railroad trestle spanning the dry riverbed. The very riverbed that just moments ago had tried to end Richard's life via the quicksand trap would now present another damned-if-you-do-and-damned-if-you-don't conundrum.

The fourth and final near-death experience in New Mexico involved a train. It was not a train one remembered as a three-year-old child. This was serious stuff, and only the Good Lord knows how they survived. The four boys started over the trestle, when, about halfway across the span, having entered the killing zone, they sensed something behind them. Turning, they saw a behemoth, serpentine train bearing down on them. They were dumbfounded, frozen in fear, as the death machine took dead aim at them.

The poor train engineer lay on his horn, realizing he was about to extinguish the four lives. Knowing they could not outrun the fast-approaching train and realizing the bridge was too high for them to jump, they had only one option, and it was not a good one. Managing to inch to the edge of the wooden railroad ties, sitting and seeing the horror on the face of the engineer, and feeling the blast of air as the train passed just inches from sending the boys into the next dimension will forever be remembered. The buffeting of the air, trying its best to push the boys to their doom, was awful. However, at that time, the fair-haired golden child realized he did indeed have nerves of steel. To panic was to die. He would draw upon this lesson later in life during other life-and-death experiences.

The mile-long train finally passed, allowing the boys to weakly wobble to the other side.

Looking back now, Richard can see how the Lord was protecting him even as a naive ten-year-old kid. Eventually leaving the wilds of New Mexico, the family returned to the safe environs of home.

CHAPTER 6

Drive, Hay, Jay

Between ages eleven and twelve, Richard learned how to drive, with much credit going to his uncle Jay. Jay was a big man who laughed easily and expected obedience from those around him. He was foreman on a large ranch outside Bakersfield, California, near Tehachapi and Weedpatch. During summers, young Richard would spend two or three weeks with Uncle Jay and Aunt Easter. Oh, how he enjoyed these times of freedom, smelling the hay and seeing the fields of cotton. It was like a coming-of-age moment. He and Uncle Jay would get up at about four thirty in the morning, and the two of them would travel by pickup truck to whatever fields of hay needed mowing or baling. Feeling grown up, Richard sat beside Jay, getting ready to do men's work; there really was not much to talk about.

When they arrived at the job site, almost on cue, Jay would say, "Darn, I forgot such-and-such. Richard, take the truck to the warehouse, and ask the guys there to give you this particular gadget."

Flooded with excitement, clambering behind the wheel, Richard was suffused with pride. Uncle Jay had confidence in the lad, knowing he was capable of driving the ten-mile round-trip journey. Coaxing the stick transmission into action, grinding a few gears, he was off.

His uncle, it seemed, had more confidence in the boy than his own father did. Jay looked at the boy as the son he'd never had.

Back at the work site, with dawn just reddening the horizon and with his full heart bursting with joy, Richard was given the work assignment. Uncle Jay would instruct on operating the machinery. He would tell Richard to mow a particular field, as he would be baling in the next. Given minimal instructions, Richard was off to his assigned task. He stopped only for lunch and usually finished the day at about five or six o'clock. Tired at the end of the day, Richard went to bed early, recounting that day's adventures.

However, not every remembrance was pleasant, as in recalling his encounter with an enraged bull corralled in a pen. For some unfathomable reason, the boy thought it great sport to badger and torment this creature to the point that it charged the fence only to be repulsed by the high electrical current running through a wire. Young Richard would unmercifully tease and provoke the animal as it repeatedly charged the fence in an effort to get to the boy. Rather smug and safe on the other side of the fence, Richard wondered at the power of the invisible force coursing through the wire. Based on earlier experiences, such as putting metal forks into electric outlets as a small child, he knew this fence was not something to be trifled with. He knew better than to touch the fence with bare hands; something was needed between hand and fence for insulation purposes. He chose the lid off a discarded tin can.

He gently touched the wire—and had an immediate sense that he'd made a rather large error. With a flash of white light, Richard was on his backside, feeling weak and nauseated.

The bull, with a look of satisfaction on its bemused face, simply walked away. On the other hand, Richard, at the moment, was not walking anywhere but was lying on his back, trying to jump-start his heart back into a normal rhythm. He spent the remainder of the day on the couch, eating saltine crackers, sipping small amounts of water, and contemplating the mysteries of electricity.

Cataloging these adventures, he moved into his twelfth year with an explosion of hormones taking his body hostage. No explanations were proffered except those gleaned from peers. However, Mother thought it wise to have Shirley and Richard stay home one Saturday, forcing upon them books, articles, and pictures explaining in some detail what was happening to their bodies. Richard, being rather prudish, was mortified as Mother asked if there were any questions at the end of this torture session. "No," Richard said, and he raced to escape. That was the end of the dreaded sex talk involving adults.

On the cusp of manhood, burdened with poor body image and low self-esteem, with an aching sense of modesty, he knew he was abnormal. He pushed much of his self-awareness down to a deeper, darker abode. As a result, he developed a Janus personality of openness and secretiveness, which has been his modus operandi for much of his life.

Before beginning high school, Richard experienced an unusual event that for some reason impacted him. On a family vacation to Northern California, his dad decided to make a brief stop to visit an acquaintance of his whom the rest of the family did not know. The man's home was a cattle ranch, and he had a son Richard's age. The two families were inside the home, visiting, when the kid instructed Richard to follow him as he went outside. What followed was unbelievable.

Richard dutifully obeyed, heading out the door. The destination was a corral housing a large bull. Without saying more than "Watch this," the insane boy aimed his .22 rifle at the bull's large scrotum, squeezing off a round. The bullet went straight through the poor bull's pride and joy. Richard watched in disbelief as the bull bellowed and became gracefully airborne. Pirouetting and landing upon its four feet, the confused and now frothing-at-the-mouth animal went into full beast mode. The insane boy, standing beside his guest, laughed maniacally, obviously proud of his marksmanship. How was this dastardly deed going to be explained away?

Precisely at that moment, both families were exiting the house, tendering their goodbyes. Richard quickly climbed into the backseat. As they drove away, Richard heard the boy's father say to his son, "It looks like something might be wrong with my bull."

Safely down the road, convinced the psychopathic kid had blamed his guest for the shooting, Richard had his first glimpse into a mendacious mind. How else could the kid explain away the destruction of the prized animal, except to blame Richard?

The imagination runs wild in thinking about what might have become of that boy.

CHAPTER 7

Early High School

Richard's first job, at age thirteen, was delivering newspapers house to house in his neighborhood. This was no simple task. It required running a gauntlet of feral dogs determined to do great bodily injury four days a week. To foil the dogs' plans, he enlisted his buddy Jerry, whose task was to ward off the beasts, waging battle from his bike. The arrangement worked well.

The stack of papers was dropped off at Richard's house at about four thirty in the morning, at which time Jerry and Richard would fold them, put rubber bands around them, and load them into two saddlebags on Richard's bike. They would begin their appointed rounds, with skinny Richard pedaling and weaving while tossing the papers using his less-than-muscular arms. Pudgy Jerry would do battle with the roving bands of dogs, allowing his pal a safe throwing lane. To any casual observer, it must have been an odd scene: skinny and fatty working harmoniously. After delivery, the young entrepreneurs would each return home to eat breakfast before going to school.

Once a month, Richard went to collect payment from each household, succeeding about 75 percent of the time in collecting the $1.75 fee. This was frustrating work with little reward. It was Richard's first exposure to people's stinginess and dishonesty. Both boys received about fifteen dollars per month, plus cheap prizes. After many months of performing this menial labor, Richard resigned and slept in for those three hours.

He did not stay unemployed long, as his uncle Jay now owned a service station and hired him to work weekends and some evenings, paying a decent wage. He did this until about age sixteen, at which time another job opportunity became available. Since he was now in possession of his own car, it was possible for him to deliver chicken dinners. For some reason, he thought delivering the dinners would be more exotic than working at the service station. It wasn't. He learned to loathe the job, as it required him to do everything: bread the chicken, fry it, take orders over the phone, prepare the meals, and deliver said product to homes. This was all before GPS or Google Maps, so it was a nightmare to locate most addresses and navigate the traffic maze to the homes. Since the busiest hours were at dinnertime, many dinners arrived late and cold. Customers were unhappy, which did not incentivize tipping. He still harbors unpleasant memories of the jingle "Don't cook tonight; call Chicken Delight." This employment lasted until graduation from high school.

Other jobs were mundane, including chores around the house and all yard work. He never had any help in the latter chore, and his father expected a perfect result. The early mower was a push type, and all edging was accomplished using a shovel. It usually took him half a day on Saturday to finish.

Once a year, he and Dad would make the pilgrimage to the local dairy farms to purchase a trailer full of cow manure, which was then spread over the Saint Augustine lawn. This always resulted in the grass being burned. It took weeks for the lawn to recover and for the odor to abate. Richard could never figure out this seasonal ritual of his father.

Richard found his stride in high school and was a good student. Teachers liked him, as he was a compliant, mildly brownnosing charge, but he was not such a brownnoser as to be disliked by his peers. Being a freshman at Excelsior High in Norwalk was fraught with challenges. Freshmen were quickly introduced to their rights as first-year plebes, which basically distilled down to no rights. Hazing was in fashion and was a new experience for Richard. Most of the hazing was good-natured, such as raw eggs placed under armpits and peeled bananas placed between buttocks, all designed to embarrass. A favorite was tying a string to a boy's private member, snaking the string under the shirt, and exiting it at the top button. The string was tied to a pencil. The goal was to get as many girls as possible to autograph a notebook with said pencil. The catch, however, was that the string was too short, necessitating the girls' bending over to give themselves enough string to sign the book. But there was never enough string, so as the girls tugged on the cord, it caused botheration, making the boy wince and the girls giggle.

One blue-eyed, blond-headed budding Nazi of German descent truly enjoyed schadenfreude. It was his truculent style to inflict maximum pain upon the new students by hitting, striking with paddles, and making people duckwalk everywhere. To be sure, he went on to become a successful Nazi or some god-awful commandant in a gulag prison.

Overall, the four years in high school were imbued with pleasant memories.

CHAPTER 8

—⁓m⁓—

High School Deeper Dive

During high school, lifelong friendships were developed, some of which lasted more than sixty years. When these friends passed on to the next life, some early and some late, each carried a small piece of Richard's heart. The time spent in high school seemed forever, a special slice in one's life. Everything was so acute, important, and in the moment. Time was spent attending football and other sporting events, always cheering for the perennial losing teams. The Hispanic star running back fractured his neck, which forever sentenced him to a life as a perpetual child. The tragedy had a great impact on all at the moment, and all vowed never to forget his name. This good intention lasted for only a few years, until eventually, none could remember his name or what became of him.

Richard's group of friends, it turned out, were popular: athletes, student council members, and debate club aficionados. They even were accepted by the bad boys. Navigating through this slightly contumacious group of people, Richard developed a persiflage personality. The boys, at lunchtime, would stand about eating chili dogs while fine-tuning words of imprecation, cursing like sailors. The more erudite of the wordsmiths could curse one or two minutes straight, seldom using a word twice. These sharp-witted, acid-tongued cursers could painlessly cut the legs out from under a person; the victim usually was the last to know. Richard, as long as the invective was not directed toward him, enjoyed this obstreperous band of boys, who meant no one harm.

He was a Goody Two-shoes around his family and teachers but was also learning the ways of the world, which fed his alter ego. Perfecting these two approaches enabled him to reconcile his increasingly conflicted beliefs about life. One worldview had a Christian slant; the other had a more secular position. There were certain things he did not want his parents to know, such as the time he received multiple swats delivered by paddle to his backside via the physical education coach. A group of boys were horsing around and were late in getting outside to the practice field. Warned of the consequences, the boys ambled out about two minutes late. They were met by the coach, who, without cunctation, ordered the perps back inside, where he instructed them to remove their gym shorts and bend over as he swatted each with a large paddle. Each blow to the bare buttocks brought pain and botheration. Wanting to cry but daring not, Richard was filled with shame.

Shaming can be a useful tool for learning, if used properly. The woke scolds now instruct people that shaming has no place in a civilized society. But of course, they are wrong, as they usually are on most subjects. Richard knew he deserved the spanking, and adding shame to the mix strengthened his resolve to never again repeat this particular transgression. Placing miscreants into public stocks in the olden days dissuaded poor behavior, thus elevating civility. This type of punishment should be meted out with compassion and would surely be frowned on today.

Every now and then, his better nature was challenged. Believing billingsgate would elevate his social standing and being a capable student, he learned to swear. There were a few times in his life when he was aware of grace brushing across his face; one time occurred when he was sixteen years old, while working on his car.

A young man from church came to his house to help him. While the young man was working on the car and instructing about auto mechanics, Richard was perfecting his cussing. After a while, the man stopped working and said, "Richard, you're better than that; you do not need to curse."

What a profound statement for Richard to hear. He'd just assumed the man was a Christian hypocrite like himself and also swore. Again, he was humbled and ashamed, and at that moment, he stopped swearing. Someday when he meets this saintly young man again, Richard will thank him for his gentle rebuke.

Basically, in high school, he was learning about the ways of the world. There was not a firm enough foundation in his family unit or a meaningful involvement in a church to act as an effective counterweight against the world's wiles.

All people are bent toward sin and away from God. This is just people's lot. It is evident that most sin feels good at the moment, which is why people do it. The only hope against this sickness is to be inoculated by Christ and His inscripturated Word. Richard was a carnal Christian until age forty-eight.

In high school, Richard was introduced to alcohol. Both his parents were teetotalers and disapproved of his budding romance with the devil water. His friends consumed the spirits with many activities, being lubricated by alcohol.

This illicit love affair with the red-eye hooch had only negative consequence on his life. He was true on one hand and hypocrite on the other. This assiduously crafted chicanery was his modus operandi for many years, but there was a cost to it.

As school progressed, he realized he was a pretty good student. He made good grades and liked to learn new information. So Richard settled into a comfortable routine of being a diligent student during the week but sneaking out his bedroom window at night and running with his buddies on the weekend. His routine was to obey instructions to be home and in bed by ten o'clock, but in fact, he was out the window by ten thirty.

It is almost certain the parents eventually caught on to the shenanigans, but no word was ever spoken concerning this trespass. The parents probably did not want to know; therefore, they did not need to deal with it. This is not good parenting, but it was great for the perpetrator as he honed his skill of duplicity. There was also a code of secrecy among all; everyone had secrets, and tattletales were frowned upon. The sisters covered for their brother and vice versa. A culture of deception was benignly nurtured. Only decades later could this be talked about and nervously laughed at.

If you live long enough, hopefully you learn a few things. Secrets are almost never good. The truth will always come out, so it's best to be as transparent as you can. Certainly, there are times to hold information in confidence with revelations being age appropriate, but out and out deception is wrong. Flaunting of rules and rank disobedience should never be rewarded with a code of silence. The idea of not being a snitch may sound honorable, but it is basically unwise. Exposing others' offenses might just save them from misery or worse. It makes sense to at least bring others into the conversation to get their perspective on a matter.

After it was all said and done, Richard continued to sneak around, drinking too much and engaging in risky behavior. In essence, he was a typical teenager of the time. Now, the word *teenager* is an American construct coined after World War II. Prior to that point, there was no such thing as a teenager; kids reached a certain age, and they were either married, working, off to war, or attending higher education. But the postwar baby boomers settled on the notion of retarding maturation by prolonging childhood. Voilà! Children up to at least age nineteen had the wanton luxury of forever being young. Today that age has lengthened to at least thirty years old for many, with the approval and indulgence of adults. Men should be men well before thirty, but instead, often, we have only boys who shave. Much could be and has been written about this teenage phenomenon, but suffice to say, this experiment has not worked out well for society.

CHAPTER 9

───w───

Digressions

A few digressions in Richard's life were of interest. The first was his exposure to the chemical cyanide, which was obtained from a metal canister mailed to his father by a relative in Oklahoma. Sending a deadly chemical through the mail surely violated many rules, but this did not dissuade Mr. Patterson. These little white pellets were used in executions. Dropping the pellets into water caused a gas to form. That's where the term *gas chamber* originated. People were executed in gas chambers across the nation, and Richard was now in possession of this product. He was about twelve years old and obviously did not understand the dangers.

His father obtained the chemical for the sole purpose of killing red ant mounds, and Richard knew where his father had hidden it in the garage. Before his dad could use it, Richard was poised to do a preemptive strike on the mounds. It was a sunny day, and Richard was the only one at home. He bent over the first mound, dropping a few pellets onto the target. Fumes immediately arose, entering his lungs as he took a breath. This caused him to reel mercifully backward away from the mound, and thus, his life was saved. Cyanide is such a potent poison that only two to four breaths in a grown man is fatal. If he had pitched forward onto the mound, it would have been the end for little Richie and this narrative. Providence was again on display.

He reported this mishap to his parents, which resulted in the cyanide being removed from the premises. To this day, how it was disposed of remains a mystery; the disposal certainly was not EPA approved.

The second digression involved a septic system. For years, his home operated on a septic system before being connected to the city sewage system. The septic contrivance consisted of a large hole in the ground lined with bricks and vented by a small pipe leading to the surface. After years of the system's disuse, Richard's dad had the ungodly idea that Richard should descend into this vile pit for a so-called inspection. With much coaxing, cajoling, and outright threats, Richard agreed.

The chamber was opened, and Richard descended with flashlight into the Machiavellian mudhole for a look. As his dad, safely atop the turf, shouted instructions to his son in the subterranean chamber, Mother appeared. The boy was quickly retrieved from the hole as Father got another dressing down by Mother. Being the mama bear, she unleashed scathing instructions to Bill about how he might improve his parenting skills. Putting his only son down a dank hole was not a good path to be on. Dad dutifully listened and melted into the shadows chagrined but unrepentant.

Richard never had thought about the cavern in the ground until Father brought it to his attention, but afterward, Richard enlisted the help of his buddy Jerry to perform an experiment: What would happen if they poured a gallon of white naphtha, or unleaded gasoline, down the vent pipe and then struck a match over the hole? Jerry volunteered to light this homemade bomb, which he did while bending over the hole. The first two attempts failed, so moving closer to the vent, he lit the third and fateful match. The ensuing explosion and fireball knocked Jerry backward, singeing his eyebrows and most of the hair on his bowling-ball-shaped head. The familiar stench of burned hair hung over the area as both boys scurried inside their homes.

The third digression involved a rabid dog. Richard had a dog named Kurt, a friendly Doberman pinscher who was always giving the dogcatcher fits. Truly, it was a cartoonish scene when the catcher arrived in front of the house and started chasing Kurt around and around his vehicle with a net held high until Kurt, tiring of the sport, escaped under the toolshed in the backyard and refused to reemerge until the catcher and net were gone. It was entertaining to witness.

Richard one day was on top of the garage roof, helping his dad apply shingles, when he spotted an aggressive dog coming down the street. The animal was foaming at the mouth. After climbing down the ladder to safely secure Kurt, Richard scrambled back up the ladder just as the poor rabid dog crashed into the fence. It was terrifying to witness, as the animal was out of control and obviously suffering. Richard's dad stated the obvious: "Just stay up here on the roof, and it will be all right." Even at a tender age, the boy could understand this wisdom. Soon thereafter, animal control captured the animal, something they never succeeded in concerning Kurt.

His dad had a poorly thought-out plan to electrify the backyard's chain-link fence by running an electric wire to the fence and plugging it into an electrical outlet. This was designed to discourage Kurt from climbing over the fence.

It worked, but there were unforeseen consequences to humans that did not appear to be on Dad's radar. Once again, Mom intervened, restoring sanity and telling Dad his plan lacked certain nuances and appeared to be poorly thought out.

Another time, Dad told his ten-year-old son to crawl under the house to perform an inspection on the cast-iron plumbing coursing under the home. This structure was built on pier and beams, so it was raised off the ground about two feet and was accessible by a small screened opening. Well, the boy had a healthy fear of anything arachnid, with spiders topping the list. The black widow spider, with its patented red hourglass design on the abdomen, was ubiquitous. Richard protested vigorously, entreating his father not to send him on this likely suicide mission. Just a cursory glance revealed interlacing spiderwebs occupying the entire space beneath the house. But there was no use in arguing: the boy was going in.

Equipped with a flashlight, with Dad standing outside barking orders, Richard entered the mausoleum, with its various desiccated dead animals and the ever-present spiderwebs interlaced among all. Dad asked for information concerning the plumbing and the condition of the pier and beams, and Richard dutifully relayed the requisite information. It seemed like forever before Dad was satisfied and allowed his young son to escape back into the glorious sunshine of the living. Richard wondered through the years if his dad really liked him. Dad, of course, said he would have done the inspection himself but was too large to crawl under the house. Just one more odd request of the patriarch.

The final vignette concerned Disneyland. It was 1955, and Disneyland was now open—what utter joy and excitement for a ten-year-old boy who dreamed of someday entering that magical theme park. Admission was one dollar for adults and fifty cents for a child under age twelve. Each ride was between twenty-five and thirty cents, which put some pressure on lower-income families, such as Richard's. However, his mom somehow saved about twenty dollars, promising the kids that they would be going. The only rub was that they had no transportation. Fortunately, the aforementioned Uncle Bill, the storyteller, came forward, offering to drive all in his chariot, a small green English Ford. By the time they left home, it was saddled with eleven people: Uncle Bill and Auntie, Mom, Richard and his two siblings, and Aunt Lily with her four rambunctious boys. Eleven people stacked like sardines wobbled slowly down the Santa Ana Freeway to Anaheim, our destination, a piece of heaven.

We pulled into the free parking lot, and thus started the highly choreographed operation of disembarking from the chariot, which took a number of minutes to accomplish. Onlookers streaming to the entrance of the park were amazed at the performance, believing it might be the first act staged by Disneyland: the always funny clown-car act. But this was normal real-life fare for Richard and his poor relations. They couldn't have cared less what they looked like to onlookers as they all raced to see what wonderments awaited. It was, just as Richard had imagined, a truly magical day.

CHAPTER 10

———~m~———

Friends

Richard had a great time hanging out with friends in high school, including having bonfires at the beach, cruising in muscle cars, having food fights, and being just responsible enough to stay out of serious trouble. His best friends were Dennis Thorpe, Bobby Jones, Bobby Milks, Doug Davis, and Ron Schoors. These friendships lasted and deepened from at least high school—some from elementary school. Four of these fellows have passed away. Dennis died in the Vietnam War (a poem about that can be found at the end of this book). Bobby Milks died from alcoholism, Ron died from cardiac disease, and Doug died from suicide. Richard loved each of these men, and when they died, they took part of his heart with them. His special love for Dennis and Bobby Jones is similar to that of King David and Johnathan, as spoken of in the Bible. Attending Dennis's funeral with full military honors was gut-wrenching and had a profound impact on Richard's life going forward.

Most of the fun involved good-natured bantering and just goofing around. One time, at Bob's Big Boy restaurant on Whittier Boulevard in Whittier, an epic food fight spontaneously broke out in Ron's new baby-blue Chevelle. The carhop brought the order of hamburgers, fries, and milkshakes. Ron was tall and fluctuated between three hundred and four hundred pounds. He was husky and big-boned—in essence, a large, fat man. He was funny and was always looking to start something.

After the food was delivered by the carhop, Ron started to pass it around to Richard, Dennis, and Jones. He thought it would be great sport if he started pouring the milkshakes onto the lap of Jones, who was sitting shotgun next to him. Of course, the counterattack was swift, with hamburgers, french fries, and milkshakes flying throughout the interior of the car. The inside of the car was trashed, no food was eaten, and people looking on in other cars were taken aback. The poor carhop came back to see if they needed anything and suppressed a small gasp as she surveyed the scene. She asked if the window tray had fallen, and could she bring a new order? The miscreants, who were dying laughing, said no, thanks, and assured her it was not her fault, and they would be on their way.

A while later, again on Whittier Boulevard, the axle-grease melee occurred, forever becoming part of the lore. Large Ron started the fracas, as he usually did. He pulled his car into a convenience store parking lot so he could go fetch a jumbo bottle of soda.

The store was located next to a service station. All sensed Ron was up to no good as he walked into the store. The three passengers bailed out of the car, and Bobby Jones presciently entered the service station service bay, deftly filled both hands with heavy axle grease, and walked back toward the car.

Ron exited the store, vigorously shaking a large bottle of soda, trying his best to douse his friends with the sticky liquid. As he chased the three while maniacally laughing, they adroitly stayed out of his way, suggesting he stop the nonsense and let all back into the car. Satisfied that he had accomplished an amazing feat, he allowed his passengers back inside the car. Richard was sitting shotgun, which was rare, with Jones and Dennis in the backseat. As big Ron was chortling, driving down Whittier Boulevard, satisfied with his immense win, Jones, sitting directly behind Ron the behemoth, calmly pressed both hands filled with the axle grease firmly into Ron's ears. This forced the heavy grease deep into Ron's ear holes.

The joy inside the car erupted as deaf, wild-eyed Ron started processing this new information. Large Ron started trying his best to pummel skinny Richard next to him with potentially lethal blows. Ron, being somewhat of a lovable coward, did not attack Bobby, the obvious culprit; he attacked the much smaller Patterson, who obviously had nothing to do with the assault. As the car slowed, Richard thought it prudent to exit the moving vehicle, taking his chances with the pavement rather than with this flailing beast. Amid curses and imprecations hurled at all, a nervous cease-fire ensued. Richard regained entry back into the car unharmed, and the quartet journeyed the fifteen miles back to Norwalk. Ron's world was silent on the cacophonous ride home. He regained most of his hearing in about one month but always blamed Richard for the fracas.

Ron was the genesis of many stories. Dennis, Richard's best friend, was half Native American and happened to be strong and athletic. Ron, on the other hand, was large and doughy, and he had an unhealthy fear of Dennis, especially if Dennis had access to firewater, guns, or swords. Many times, Ron would drive to Dennis's home, exit his car, walk toward the front door, and then notice that the small hole in the screen on the window was occupied by the muzzle of a pellet rifle. Too late to avoid it, he was once again caught in no-man's-land, a.k.a. the killing zone. Dennis would give instructions to Ron to the effect of "If you take one more step or if any of your fatness moves, I will shoot you." This was funny indeed. Ron would threaten and begin a steady stream of invectives, discussing the entire lineage of Dennis's ancestry, which always resulted in a fusillade of flying pellets penetrating Ron's ample flesh.

Eventually making it to the front door by navigating a circuitous route, Ron would let himself in. Howling to high heaven, he would detail his plans for how to handle this heathen, and Dennis, coming out of his room laughing, would announce, "It is now belly-beating time." Hearing this dreadful news, Ron always wilted, and before long, the half-crazed Indian had his 165 pounds astraddle his victim's 300-plus pounds. He would commence slapping and spanking Ron's ponderous panniculus while Ron did his best imitation of a beetle on its back, flailing arms and legs. This was immensely entertaining.

Eventually tiring of this display of alpha dominance, Dennis would get off Ron, allowing him to roll over and begin to stand. But the next scene was even more diabolical, with Dennis now in possession of a genuine Samurai sword. He would make thrusting, parrying, and stabbing movements directed toward Ron in an attempt to pin the behemoth beetle to the floor. Usually, at this point, spectators would intervene, halting the ritualistic display, allowing everything to return to normal. Everybody laughed, even Ron, but he always harbored a fear of Indians.

As mentioned, usually, Ron was the instigator, as during an episode that occurred in Richard's second year of college. Ron never attended college but started driving a truck delivering Bubble Up and various other sodas to stores. In spite of his driving the truck off the end of Huntington Beach Pier due to "loss of brakes," he was promoted, eventually becoming a regional director of Pepsi Company. Dennis was a few years from joining the army and becoming a Green Beret. Dennis and Richard enjoyed climbing mountains and exploring caves, mines, or any large hole in the ground.

On this adventure in Nevada, the two of them located an abandoned, locked-down mine. They were able to gain entrance and invited Ron to join in the exploration. Ron, who did not like to climb mountains or descend into holes in the ground, politely declined.

Ron would await the explorers back at camp. He was given instructions that if the two were not back by dusk, it was likely something ill had befallen them, and he should notify the authorities. Of course, he ignored the specific instructions.

So engrossed in exploring the mine, the two lost track of time. Exiting the mine, they were surprised to see that it was well past dusk. The night was illumined by a full moon, so there was no reason for their lanterns to be lit. This was a near-fatal mistake as they approached the camp while amiably chatting about their adventure. They saw Ron sitting in the trunk of his car, which had been backed up to a roaring fire. He was cradling his repeat .22 rifle and was staring into the fire toward the mine. Blinded by the fire, the dummkopf yelled, "Who goes there?" and he started squeezing off round after round, not waiting for an answer to his inquiry. Dennis and Richard were yelling as Ron was firing. Thankfully, no harm was inflicted, but it was the first time Richard heard bullets whizzing by his head. Of course, name-calling ensued.

There were many other stories to emerge from that time in Richard's life. While the boys were driving one night from Whittier to Norwalk, Dennis and Bob Jones were sitting in the backseat of Ron's car, when horseplay broke out, resulting in Jones's letterman jacket being thrown out the back window. Never one to let such an

THE REST OF ME

opportunity pass, Ron stopped the car and proceeded to drive back and forth over the garment, pressing it firmly into the pavement. Under the threat of death, Ron stopped the car, and the jacket was retrieved. Bobby and Dennis got into a kerfuffle, with both guys grabbing the other's genitalia and squeezing. This was awesome to witness, providing Ron and Richard with much entertainment on the twelve-mile ride to Norwalk. Both spectators encouraged the combatants to squeeze harder and dare not trust the other to let go first. Ha, what fun. Ron pulled up to the local pool hall, and Richard raced inside to announce the arrival of the glorious genitalia gladiators. The pool hall immediately emptied as the patrons surrounded the arena, a.k.a. the car. They encouraged the gladiators to increase the squeeze and dare not let go. My gosh, it was funny to witness. Just before passing out, both contestants were coaxed to release their death grips on the count of three, which they did. This episode immediately became legend.

One might think this book is about Ron Schoors, as he is such a treasure trove of material to mine. Everyone liked Ron, who laughed easily at himself and others, making it fun to be around him. Richard, Dennis, and Ron traveled to the Salton Sea one day to drink beer and shoot guns. This is always a bad combination, except when dove hunting in Texas in September, when cold beer is a necessity. On this outing, Dennis, as usual, consumed too much of the red-eye and quickly transformed into an Indian brave searching for a scalp. Per usual, that someone was poor ponderous Ron. Dennis and Richard had ascended a hill, discovering a small cave. Ron, not wanting to exert himself without cause, lingered in a dry riverbed, when the invitation was proffered by Dennis to come climb the hill and join the explorers. Naively and unbelievably, Ron accepted the invitation and started hauling his husk up the hill. Richard, not having a gun, was a mere observer, sitting next to Dennis, who was softly chuckling to himself.

Halfway up the climb, Ron calculated too late his mistake. Dennis stood, raining verbal abuse upon his head, and started pinging at Ron's feet with his one-shot .22 rifle, demanding Ron perform a dance routine. Ron, now totally engaged and not in the mood to perform a dance, started spraying the area around the heads of his tormentors with his repeat .22 rifle. With bullets whizzing around and overhead, Ron started a slow retreat by rolling and tumbling down the hill to the safety of the riverbed. Hugging the near bank afforded him some cover, except for his ample buttocks protruding some six inches above the riverbank, presenting Dennis a clear shot. With Richard ducking, Dennis tried his best to kick dirt upon Ron's backside with his single shot, while Ron was cursing like a sailor with a debut of new words, all the while lying down covering fire. It was quite a sight. It was fun for a while, until Dennis ran out of ammunition, and a cease-fire was called. Ron emerged with his bottom tattooed with dirt, totally spent of any remaining foul language in his repertoire. Sobered by time and sunshine, they all agreed it was foolish, and it was providential that nobody was injured. But it was funny and destined to be enshrined in their lexicon of lore.

Two other friends were Bobby Milks and Doug Davis. Milks was somewhat of a tragic comedic character. Friend to Richard since elementary school, he was the youngest of four brothers and a sister. Nice looking, a talented athlete, and a good dancer, he made friends easily. He was stubborn and loved to gossip but was also fun-loving.

Good times usually involved Bobby Milks, Jones, Dennis, Schoors, and Richard.

In junior high and high school, the sky seemed to be the limit for Bobby; however, as is always the case, life got in the way. Escaping an abusive father, Milks joined the army and appeared to be on a good road. While deployed to Korea, he received news his father had suddenly died. He was recalled from Korea and was honorably discharged so he could care for his mother. His siblings did not want the responsibility, so being the person he was, he stepped forward to care for her. His mother saw herself as a victim and became totally dependent on Bobby, forever changing the trajectory of his life.

Hardworking and a good provider, he began smoking and drinking to excess. Gradually becoming more reclusive, he became like a poor man's Howard Hughes, unkempt and isolated, growing his hair and nails long. He pretty much refused to interact with any of his old friends. He worked and used up his life on caring for his mother, who outlived him. The last time Richard saw Bobby, he was about fifty years old, looking disheveled and embarrassed his friend saw him in that condition. Shortly thereafter, he passed away. His was an unrequited life greatly mourned by all his many friends.

Another friend of Richard's who lived an unfulfilled life was Doug Davis. He had a difficult childhood and lived life hard, battling his entire life against alcoholism. He was one of the few friends, with the other being Bobby Jones, who was not at all impressed with Richard's academic achievements, calling BS on all his latest fads and ideas. Richard had a good relationship with him, but after losing his beloved wife, Sue, to cancer at an early age, Doug started withdrawing into his own world of alcohol and separation, taking the unprecedented step of moving from Southern California to

Arizona, eschewing his friends. He would call Richard, who was living in Texas, late at night, talking nonsense peppered with foul language. Jones, Richard, and others became concerned, as he began evincing suicidal ideation; even trips by Jones to Arizona could not dissuade him from taking his own life. Everyone felt helpless and impotent.

One by one, Richard lost his boyhood friends: Dennis to war, Ron to heart disease, Bobby Milks to alcoholism, and Doug to suicide. His only remaining California boyhood friend is Bobby Jones. But at seventy-five years of age, we are flying over the drop zone, and the doors may open on us at any time. Friends are a rare gift and should never be presumed upon. Included at the end of the manuscript are poems addressing the topic of friends.

CHAPTER 11

—m—

Snakes and Bats

As time does, it passed. Richard finished junior college, and life became somewhat more serious. During summers and holidays, he worked at Douglas Oil refinery, where his father was employed. He was earning about fifteen dollars per hour, which was a good wage. He saved most of the money to fund his education. Changing majors from geology to forest management and, finally, zoology with a minor in chemistry resulted in five years of college. He lived at home, commuting to school, and life settled into a predictable routine: school and study during the week and working and relaxing or partying on the weekend. A number of events happened between 1963 and 1972, impacting all. The Vietnam War was in full bloom, and a number of friends had been drafted or had enlisted. Since there was a draft lottery, a low number selected almost guaranteed that you would be drafted. Richard's number was 56 out of 365, which augured poorly for him. During that time, he was still very much involved in his zoological studies.

He had become friends with classmate Lynn Robbins, who was an expert herpetologist and was eager to teach Richard all he knew about field zoology and the art of capturing and preserving animals. Many weekend days or nights, they were in the fields, ponds, deserts, or mountains, capturing animals for studies. At night, running the desert roads was productive in capturing many reptiles.

Richard had observed his friend many times capturing rattlesnakes, including the serpentine sidewinder. He was an eager, capable assistant, a position comfortable to him. It never occurred to him that he would ever be called upon to capture a rattlesnake himself. However, upon locating a five-foot-long *Crotalus crotalus* (a western diamondback rattlesnake) one day, Lynn announced this would be a good time for Richard's maiden flight.

After restarting his heart, Richard wanted to choose flight over fight, but after screwing up what little courage he had, he rose to the challenge. Using his hooked snake tool, he managed to pull the serpent from under the boulder he had just been sitting on. To say the animal was peeved and ready for battle would be a disservice to the moment. Pinning the head to the ground using the snake tool, Richard nervously inched his right hand just behind the head of the reptile. So far so good, but alas, then came the near-fatal error. The nuanced move Richard had not learned was critical: the snake is picked up, and the arm is held out away from one's body as the serpent is dropped into a gunnysack that is quickly tied. Richard, not having learned this maneuver, picked up the reptile while holding his arm straight up, not away from his body, thus allowing the snake to wrap its muscular five-foot-long body around Richard's arm. Who had whom? The reptile was writhing, trying to pull away from Richard's weakening death grip on its neck. Yellowish venom was dripping from its fangs. Richard was struggling to unwind the snake's body from his arm, when his friend came to the rescue, instructing on proper technique.

With the snake finally secured, Richard marveled at the entire episode. It was an adrenaline rush crowned by exhilaration. The lesson learned was to pay attention, especially to the small details;

it could be life-saving. Richard was a quick study on how to safely capture an angry rattlesnake, a beautiful rosy boa, or a crafty chuckwalla.

Soon researchers, zoos, and various professors started requesting certain species they needed for their studies. One request was for bats, particularly vampire bats from Mexico. This necessitated traveling into Mexico and spending ten days collecting animals. What an adventure—battling a large grass fire, sharing the last case of Coors beer with the Mexicans, being invited into their dirt-floored homes to share meager meals, and sleeping in a dry riverbed with tens of thousands of daddy longlegs spiders. While sleeping, they were securely covered with plastic sheeting to ward off the predations of the dreaded vampire bats.

They discovered a large cave opening with the entrance surrounded by a large pool of water, and it was deemed a potentially good bat cave. Richard and Lynn volunteered to wade and swim the short distance to the entrance, leaving the other two with the task of setting up a mist net near the opening in the hope of ensnaring any exiting bats. Lynn and Richard entered the cave and were met with a strong odor of ammonia, indicating the presence of bat guano.

Richard, wearing an old felt safari hat, quickly became unnerved. Lynn led as they crept deeper into the cave, with the bat guano eventually reaching a knee-high depth. It was like a nightmarish scene out of a horror movie. The walls and ceiling seemed alive with cockroaches and other repulsive vermin. As the cavern narrowed, the bats became more agitated and began squeaking. Toward the end of the tunnel, Lynn thought it a splendid idea to fire off a round from his .22 pistol.

The launching of the bird shot was a bad idea, setting off a chaotic scene. The bats panicked, as did Richard, and all living things swarmed toward the cave's exit. The problem was, the explorers stood between the bats and the only exit. With bats swirling around their heads, they mustered all the nerve they could not to panic. If they stood still, bats, with their excellent sonar capabilities, avoided crashing into them. But if they tried dodging, which was a natural response, bats would invariably crash into them. It was pure terror as bats raced to the exit and cockroaches fell from the ceiling. Richard was completely unnerved upon reaching the exit and blessed sunlight. The undertaking resulted in a haul of dozens of bats, including a number of the prized vampires.

The next day, the plan was to head back to California so all could be home for Christmas. However, that night, while resting in the village of San Blas, everyone decided to trek through the jungle to Tepec, a twenty-five-mile journey. Rick, who was driving the VW bus, managed to veer off the dirt road, flipping the vehicle three times. Luckily, all were safe, but the VW was damaged. Lynn, Richard, and one other decided to start walking back toward San Blas. Again, the scene was unnerving, as they heard monkeys and other animal sounds in the dark night.

About sunup, a group of Mexican fishermen picked them up and drove them the remainder of the way to the village. The *federales* arrested Rick and put him in the caboose—not a good place to be. Per chance, the governor of the state of Sonora was visiting the village and heard about the plight of the Americanos. He intervened, and with seventy dollars being the lubricant, criminal Rick was sprung from jail. After the straightening out of fenders and various other repairs, the vehicle became operational, allowing the boys to make the slow drive back home. However, Richard needed to be back in time for Christmas so he could spend time with best friend Dennis, who was on leave from the Vietnam War, so he took a Mexican express bus, thinking it would speed him home. What a two-day journey it was—fending off hookers, swindlers, ne'er-do-wells, food vendors, and the like. Upon finally arriving in Mexicali on Christmas Eve, he walked across the bridge to Calexico, California, and was grateful for shelter, fitfully sleeping on a bench in the lobby of a urine-soaked flophouse.

At the break of dawn, he bought a Greyhound bus ticket to Los Angeles, where family picked him up and drove him home for Christmas dinner. God was gracious in orchestrating these events, allowing Richard and Dennis to spend three days together. Neither knew it would be the last earthly contact they had with each other.

Deciding they would spend three days learning to ski, off to Big Bear Lake they went. A couple of rubes, neither had any idea about skiing, but both were young and athletic, so they thought, *What could go wrong?* Plenty, it seemed. Learning the hard way, they discovered they needed gloves on their hands before grabbing a moving tow rope. Squirming, with flesh on fire, they managed to ascend to the top of the hill before unceremoniously falling at the feet of the tow-rope operator. The operator was incredulous that anyone could accomplish such a dumb feat sans gloves. So they received their first lesson: he suggested they spend a few bucks on gloves to make the outing more enjoyable. They took his advice, which made the next two days of learning the rudiments of skiing less painful.

On their arrival home, goodbyes were tendered, and both settled back into their routines. Dennis started Green Beret training, while Richard was just months away from graduation, with no real idea for future plans. Richard and his friend Lynn were selected by the Smithsonian Institute to travel to Africa for a three-year study of the nomenclature of small mammals of North Africa. It was exciting news, but alas, it was not to be for Richard. Since he had a low draft number, he was drafted into the army, while Lynn, who was a conscientious objector due to his being a member of the Jehovah's Witnesses church, got a deferment. Richard, being Baptist, was deemed desirable cannon fodder for the war. Going through an all-day physical examination, checking all the boxes, and stopping at all the stations, Richard passed and was accepted as a new army recruit. He was given orders to report to Fort Ord in Northern California for basic training. Having many friends serving in the military, he was not overly upset about going, but his mother had a different take on the matter.

Prior to being drafted, Richard was in a genetics laboratory with a classmate who indicated he had applied to dental school. Therefore, he received a deferment from the draft, as all dental, medical, pharmacy, and veterinary students were exempt. Richard, really having no desire to be a dentist but with the Smithsonian offer off the table, due to his high eligibility for the draft, decided he might as well apply for dental school. Since the hour was so late, most schools had already accepted their students for the July semester; however, Richard received offers from three out-of-state schools.

Behind the scenes and unbeknownst to him, his mother contacted their congressman, Mr. Chet Holifield. She relayed the information that Richard had been selected to attend dental school and therefore should be exempt from being drafted. Richard had no idea of these behind-the-scenes negotiations. Everything was decided by others: he was instructed to attend dental school and not the army. The confusing information was relayed to him via telephone by an unnamed and unmet general.

With so much happening that was out of his control and a bit upset about the clandestine negotiations, he decided to spend the weekend fishing with his father at Lake Isabella. It was enjoyable until we arrived home.

This was a turning point, a marker, an Ebenezer in Richard's life. Pulling into the driveway, dad and son were met by Richard's mother as the car came to a stop. Immediately, the sense came over Richard that his best friend was dead. Mother confirmed the terrible news as the world of Richard made a convulsive pivot. Not Dennis, the dashing, handsome hero of high school, coming home in a stainless-steel bucket. The talented tormentor of Ron, the friend who always blocked on Richard's blind side. Dennis, now traveling under the sable wings of night, was no more.

Depression descended upon Richard. *So what if I am still in bed? Don't be concerned for me. I am not thee. I buried old friend Dennis yesterday, running out of space in my soul, I say. Digging his grave in my heart, the least I can do on my part. Flipping a coin coming up heads, other tails, common sense fails. I have nothing figured out, no wisdom to share. One goes to heaven and one to hell.*

Anger, confusion, and sadness overwhelmed Richard; he had already lost a few friends in the war, and now Dennis. The best course of action, he reasoned at that point, was to avoid going to the Vietnam meat grinder of a war and take the option of attending dental school, as proffered by the congressman. Accepting the offer to attend Meharry Medical School of Dentistry made sense to him. It was located in Nashville, Tennessee, which was far away from California. It was inexpensive, and he knew no one there. Receiving confirmation and assurance from a brief conversation with the mysterious unnamed general, he was instructed to ignore all correspondence from the army and any threatening letters from the government. Richard registered at Meharry, beginning a new chapter in his life.

His dear friend Bobby Jones had been drafted but had the good fortune of being stationed in Germany and not Vietnam. Bobby was popular with everyone; he'd served as the class president throughout high school and been crowned homecoming king. It was nice to be his friend; he was always even-keeled, laughing easily. He was a peacemaker, a large and strong man. To this day, Richard enjoys being around him, one of his few remaining friends.

Bobby was generous to his friend Richard. They had set up a joint bank account in high school and periodically deposited money, thinking someday it might be used for a good purpose. There was about $400 in the account in 1968 when Richard left for school. Since Richard did not have much money, Bobby decided the money would be put to best use by his giving it all to Richard for expenses at school. To this day, Richard still marvels at the selfless generosity of Bobby. Of course, Richard keeps promising to pay him back someday, but Bobby just laughs at his miserly friend.

Society was in turmoil. It was 1968 when Richard started dental school. After a tearful parting at home, he put the past behind, starting anew. Always safely ensconced at home, he never had had to worry about food, shelter, or laundry. He now faced new responsibilities.

Upon arriving at Meharry, he walked into the registrar's office to sign in and receive his housing information. A kind older black lady greeted him with some astonishment in her eyes. This was an all-black school, and there standing before her was a surfer-looking white boy. What to do, and where to put this white anomaly? She quickly recovered and relaxed as the door opened as another white lad entered the room. Problem solved. Hailing from Massachusetts, David was now his new roommate.

What a culture and social change it was as this pale young man from Southern California was suddenly thrust into this black culture. It was amazing as he was quickly accepted and assimilated by his African American peers. At the end of four years, he was even elected class treasurer, a moment he cherished.

CHAPTER 12

Sundry Stories

There were many activities occurring at Meharry leveraged by student power, which was quite intoxicating. Richard was not spiritually anchored, so like any wavering reed, he was easily swayed by any reasonable-sounding argument.

He was introduced to all sorts of causes, movements, and grievances. Growing his hair longer and sporting a full beard, he became more like a counterculture hippie, even to the point of flirting with joining the Communist Party. Friends at home argued and tried to talk some sense into him when he returned home for the holidays or during summer break. Omniscient in his own eyes and condescending in attitude, he was not pleasant to be around at that point in his life. However, his core group of friends put up with him and never abandoned their friend. He navigated that tightrope of change until he graduated and moved on from that milieu of nonsense. But it was a fascinating time, and he relished the experience, as his world was expanded. Generally, most of the blacks were from upper-middle-class lineage. They were the elites, well cultured and mannered. This was in contrast to the whites' lower-middle-class status, evidenced by much boorish behavior. At parties, the brothers would be more appropriate, while the whites usually imbibed to excess. Richard was often cataloged with the boors and not the better-behaved brothers.

Many stories emerged from the time spent at Meharry, such as one student catching his hair on fire in a lab, with no one coming to his aid but an instructor, and a professor telling the entire class that no one would pass his biochemistry class. The highest score was a 47, so one could imagine the curve needed in passing the students.

One day an astounding drama unfolded. Tommy, a tall, thin black fellow student, was reputed to be quite the ladies' man. He was affable and was often seen driving around the neighborhood in his pale pink Cadillac convertible, usually accompanied by a small white poodle. Meharry was located across the street from Fisk University, a prestigious all-black liberal arts institution. The university was attended by many beautiful coeds. This cornucopia was certainly leveraged to Tommy's advantage.

The third-floor clinic was in full hum one afternoon, when two black Lincoln Continentals were spied pulling into the curved driveway and stopping at the entrance of the school. Looking down from the third-floor windows, students saw an unusual scene unfold as six large, well-suited black men exited the vehicles and entered the doors of the school. Moments later, the clinic doors opened, and they entered, inquiring about the whereabouts of Tommy. Students and faculty stood silently as the men approached a visibly shaken Tommy. The leader spoke calmly and forcefully, saying they had just arrived from Chicago with an important message: if Tommy was ever again seen cavorting or speaking with the beautiful daughter of a known black Mafia boss of Chicago, it would not end well for him. Needless to say, Tommy, not a man of deep conviction, was at the point of swooning. He staggered about as if hit by a haymaker. The men then returned to their cars and simply drove away.

The entire episode probably did not last more than three or four minutes, but it was a powerful three or four minutes. Being a wise young man, Tommy took the advice of the messengers and was never again seen anywhere in the vicinity of the Fisk beauty.

Due to a lack of resources, Richard never had a date or dined at a restaurant during his four years at Meharry. His usual fare consisted of scrambled hamburger meat with eggs, canned tuna and crackers, or a pot of pinto beans. Breakfast was easy; it was always cereal. For entertainment, he would hang out at friends' homes. For the first three years, he had roommates, with Charles, a.k.a. Tuna, being the favorite. Charlie was a neat guy from Phoenix, Arizona, who was attending medical school. He was charismatic and funny and later had a strong influence on Richard's accepting an intern position at Veterans Hospital in Houston, Texas. During his last year at Meharry, Richard lived alone, renting a basement in an old three-story house for seventy dollars per month, which included utilities and furnishings. One can imagine how nice this place was, but Richard kept it clean.

Coming home for lunch, he would sit at the kitchen table, eating tuna fish from the can, as the friendly mice sat patiently on the steam radiator, watching. No one intruded on the others' space; the polite mice knew he would leave soon, allowing them to scavenge the remains in the can. This pleasant ritual played out most days. One not-so-pleasant ritual was the constant battle waged against the enormous flying cockroaches for supremacy of the habitation. Richard became deadly accurate in the ground-to-air war with the flying demons. As a roach would scuttle across the floor or launch itself into the air, Richard, with perfect aim of Hot Shot roach spray, would blast the nasty creature into insect hell.

Two episodes occurred that reminded all of the tensions of

racism and social intolerance permeating the air of 1969–1970. During one of his numerous excursions between Norwalk and Nashville, Richard stopped at a hamburger joint on Highway 40 in Texas. Looking like Charles Manson but maybe somewhat like Jesus, sporting long hair and a full beard, he was consistently ignored and refused service. Finally, he left and was able to purchase the hamburger elsewhere, but it was his first experience with blatant discrimination.

The second time involved two black classmates, John and Warren, traveling with him to California for the Christmas holiday. The two friends were outstanding young men who later went on to stellar achievements. On that particular dark night, after refueling the car, John decided he would drive, allowing Richard to sleep in the backseat. His two friends were in the front seat, chatting, when a West Texas police car with lights flashing pulled over the car. The white police officer was disrespectful as he started to aggressively question John and Warren. However, noticing Richard, who was white, rising from the backseat seemed to confuse him a bit as he started processing this new information that did not fit his narrative. It was three o'clock in the morning when he ordered them to follow him to the justice of the peace in some Podunk town, where the judge was roused from bed to hold court. John was found guilty of speeding, and with a fine of fifty dollars, the boys were again on their way. The episode left a bad taste in Richard's mouth, as he'd witnessed the black men being disrespected.

Richard made the trip to and from Nashville a total of thirteen times. It took him forty-one hours of nonstop driving to make the sojourn. During the gas-shortage years, it was a game of roulette, going from one gas station line to another, as he traveled across the country. Many stations had no gas to sell, and some had a five-gallon limit per customer, making the experience nerve-racking and harrowing. Not having enough money for motels, Richard would sleep briefly on the side of the road before continuing the journey. The trips brought back memories of traveling from California to Oklahoma or Arkansas as a boy on annual family vacations. Leaving home with about $200, the family would commence the trip. There was no money for extras, such as fast food or motels, so all would eat white bread with a slab of bologna without chips, condiments, or drinks. They quenched their thirst by drinking water from a canvas pouch hanging from the front bumper of the car. It was as if the hillbilly Clampetts were traveling across the country. There was no air-conditioning in the car, except for a swamp cooler, which hung from the passenger-side window. All windows were usually rolled down, resulting in terrible road noise, with attendant dehydration from the constant wind. Poor Dad would drive until exhausted, pull to the side of the road, lie down on the ground for about an hour to rest, and then begin driving again. While he drove through the night, the kids would sleep: one on the backseat, one on a pallet on the floorboard, and one on the shelf behind the backseat. Richard was used to this type of travel, so he was well prepared for a long trek of forty-one hours.

Richard experienced many strange things while traveling across the country, such as being stopped in the middle of the night during a driving rain storm by a fourteen-year-old hitchhiker standing in the middle of a dark road. Of course he picked him up, asking where he was going. The boy said, "Anywhere you're going." Well, Richard was going east, and the boy wanted to go west, so Richard drove him to the interstate highway and dropped him off. The surreal moment caused Richard to wonder about the eventual well-being of the boy.

Another time, there was an unbelievable demonstration of a monstrous thunderstorm engulfing Richard at dusk one evening in West Texas. A tornado could be seen snaking itself along the ground at a distance in a downpour so intense that the rain actually found its way inside the Volkswagen. The sky was roiling with a deep felt blackness, with lightning piercing the muddy clouds and dancing on the telephone poles, with balls of fire rolling along the power lines. With hail pounding the car and visibility near zero, Richard was forced to pull to the side of the road and watch the display of nature's fury.

The car Richard drove on more than half the trips home was a VW Bug rated at forty-one horsepower; it was neither powerful nor fast. Richard devised a scheme to increase gas mileage and speed by drafting behind large eighteen-wheeler trucks. Pulling behind a big rig and staying close, he was able to coax about ten miles per hour more out of the VW. Most truckers knew what he was attempting and didn't seem to mind, but it was somewhat nerve-racking for Richard. There was a certain danger to it, but he was able to draft with a truck for many miles before losing this edge. Then, like a predator, he would locate his next victim. There was an element of challenge and fun as he tried to slingshot his way across America.

Going home for the summer break between his junior and senior years at Meharry, the VW gave up the ghost about fifteen miles east of Oklahoma City. It had been Richard's faithful chariot for many years, but its pistons were now powerless for propulsion. After coasting to the side of Interstate 40, he hitchhiked into the city and solicited the help of the aforementioned Maggie and chiropractor

Paul, who drove him to retrieve his worldly belongings from the disabled car. When they arrived at the scene, there was a kindly old gentleman sitting near the car, smoking a pipe. He'd stopped his car to check out the stranded VW to see if anyone needed assistance. Finding no one present and seeing the car filled with books and clothing, he'd deduced it was probably a student's car, and he'd thought it wise to stay with the car to deter any possible thievery. This he had done for about two hours until Richard returned. The profound act of kindness and chivalry had a lasting impact on Richard.

As for Richard's saga at Meharry, with his four years ending upon graduation and really not wanting to be a general dentist, he faced a dilemma: set up practice or continue his education. The aforementioned friend Charles had accepted an internship in ophthalmology at Ben Taub Hospital in Houston, Texas, and told Richard there was an opening at Veterans Hospital for a dental intern. Richard applied and was accepted, with employment starting July 1. He and Charles would be roommates once again, with the possibility of new adventures. After graduation, Richard and his sister Sue traveled with all his worldly possessions back to Norwalk, with a stopover in New Orleans, which neither had visited before.

Of course, there were hidden surprises awaiting them on the ostensibly mundane trip. Upon arriving in the Big Easy, Richard wanted to explore Metairie Cemetery, 150 acres of above-ground crypts and mausoleums. "It's good to visit a cemetery every now and then," he said. "It helps to center a person to the reality of life. We are on this globe for only a short period of time and should understand that everything goes back into the box." Since much of the area in the cemetery was below sea level or just a few feet above, the deceased were buried above ground in crypts. If buried below ground, the coffins would have floated to the surface due to high-level groundwater.

Driving around the grounds, Richard spotted two men working in front of one of the mausoleums. Noticing they were being watched, they motioned for the two curious onlookers to come closer. Walking to the grave site, they were met with an unusual scene: the crypt door had been opened, and a stretcher had been removed and lay on the grass with the few remains of a corpse. It was fascinating. Richard, in his thirteen years of higher education, had dissected and been familiar with three embalmed bodies; the one in dental school had been probed, prodded, and peered at over a period of nine months. But he had never seen this situation before. The crypt keepers explained that the sepulchers were all family owned, and some went back many generations, with each having shelves on which the deceased were placed. As a new death occurred, the crypt was opened, and the oldest remains were removed and deposited into a central communal pit, making room for the newest resident. What a fascinating local custom.

When they left New Orleans, Sue was driving the red Chevelle on a back road in Louisiana while Richard slept in the backseat, when all of a sudden, there was a loud banging noise. Sitting up quickly from his slumber, Richard peered out the back window and watched in amazement as the car's gas tank spun on the roadway, seemingly keeping pace with the now tankless car. It was surreal. They coasted to a stop on the side of the road, and Richard emerged from the car to retrieve the wayward tank.

After a short while, a kind fellow in a pickup truck stopped, inquiring if he could be of assistance. He drove the two bewildered people into the small town just down the road, where they consulted a mechanic, who then drove Richard to fetch the tank and the car. Upon returning to the garage, the mechanic proceeded to demonstrate the fine points of welding a damaged gas tank, or, in that case, a potential gas bomb. Certain the man had lost his Louisiana mind, Richard and his sister removed themselves from the immediate vicinity. However, the confident, calm man explained that he would first fill the tank with water, thus displacing the gasoline vapors, and then proceed to weld the defused bomb. It was a brilliant demonstration of many physical laws Richard would never have figured out.

With the tank repaired and securely strapped back onto the underside of the car and with enough gasoline to drive to the nearest station, they paid the mechanic a reasonable fee, and they were back on the road to California.

CHAPTER 13

---~ww~---

Internship and Residency

After about a three-week visit home, Richard drove to Houston and reunited with his friend Charlie. Tuna was now an intern at Ben Taub Hospital, and Richard was a new dental intern at Veterans Hospital. With his newly minted doctor of dental surgery credentials, he did not feel a real sense of accomplishment, but he did have a job paying a decent salary and translating to unlimited possibilities. Applying for the position of dental internship required the requisite résumé with attending details, but it did not require a photograph of the applicant. Therein lay the interesting rub: the hospital expected a Black man from Meharry who might give them some street cred; instead, Richard showed up for the first day of work as a long-haired, bearded white hippie, shocking all. The department chairman was visibly taken aback, expecting a trophy educated Black man, and was left stammering out a restrained welcome to the less desirable Richard. The irony was delicious as the Black and Hispanic nurses and assistants, who were also expecting a handsome dark-skinned man, eagerly and laughingly welcomed Richard. It took time for the white part of the team to get comfortable with the unanticipated curveball. It was an interesting time as Richard learned how to function and navigate in a hospital setting.

The pace was slow, nondemanding, and boring. As the intern year came to an end, Richard was offered a position as staff dentist at the hospital. That was fine since it came with a stable income, but being a general dentist was not something he desired for his future.

Richard's roommate, Charlie, moved to Dallas to continue his training. Renting an apartment, Richard settled into the staff dentist routine. During that time, he learned of the oral and maxillofacial surgery program offered at Texas Health Science Center, based out of Ben Taub Hospital. As he joined the residents on their grand rounds every Thursday morning, a new world unfolded before him. He applied for a position as a first-year resident and was accepted. Excited about landing the coveted position, Richard was informed it came with one caveat: he had to cut his hair and shave his beard. All the faculty were ex-military, and that was their politically incorrect requirement. He would have to do so before the next grand rounds occurring the next day. When he entered the room the next morning less hirsute, the place erupted in laughter and applause. The old guard had won that battle. The year was 1974, and the next four years were going to be amazing. In addition, Richard had met his future wife, Carolyn, in 1973 while still an intern at the Veterans Hospital.

Regaling all, fancying himself a raconteur, Richard narrated his weekend exploits, which were much embellished. A member of his audience was Mr. Rice, a dental technician, who introduced him to his beautiful brunette daughter, Carolyn. Courting her eventually resulted in marriage. Life was good as Richard drove around in his newly purchased yellow Porsche with the brunette beauty next to his side.

July 1974 came with Dr. Patterson, the newly appointed oral and maxillofacial surgery first-year resident, on the job. There were four first-year residents and four second-, third-, and fourth-year residents, for a total of sixteen doctors. One particular Sunday morning, Richard was scheduled to be on his first day of call, properly attired in scrubs and a white coat with his name displayed on the front. Bursting with pride, he left the parking garage early, using the staff entrance to Ben Taub Hospital, a level-one trauma center that was also the county hospital for indigent patients. Needless to say, it was a busy place.

Walking down the long hallway, not really knowing where to go or what to do, he heard a heart-stopping command from the hospital intercom: "Stat, oral surgery Three North. Stat, oral surgery Three North." Suddenly highly alert and acutely sensitive, Richard started to decode the message. First, was it really directed toward him? Yes, it appeared so, as he was the only oral and maxillofacial surgery resident on call and in the hospital at the moment. Second, with limited knowledge of most things, he somehow knew what the word *stat* meant. It meant *immediately*, as in "Hurry. Step smartly." Three North meant Three North, a place and a direction unknown at the time to little Richy. Tamping down his recently eaten breakfast and rising panic, he started processing the worrisome information. Fear gripped him as he realized there was no room for playacting; this was serious life-and-death grown-up stuff.

Realizing he knew less than nothing about nothing, he slowly meandered his way toward Three North, where he observed a group of professional-looking, no-nonsense people leaning into and attending an elderly black lady who had just experienced cardiac arrest and was now resuscitated. Seeing the crisis had passed, with the lady now alert, Richard slowly advanced, introducing himself as the new oral surgery resident. None seemed surprised, and no judgment was rendered at the revelation. Realizing the patient recently had been operated on for the repair of a fractured mandible and was now on the oral surgery service, Richard quickly busied himself in reviewing the chart, acting as if he knew things. He realized at that precise moment he had better soberly study his new profession. Performing surgery on people carried with it a grave responsibility; society was investing in Richard the ability and privilege of becoming a surgeon. This baptismal event of approximately one hour completely unnerved him as he trudged through the myriad pager calls for the next twenty-four hours.

After finally leaving the hospital at six o'clock the next evening, he quickly ate dinner and went straight to bed, exhausted, knowing he would be back at the hospital for a twelve- to fifteen-hour shift soon. Many times, he was awake for at least thirty-six hours. He repeated this routine for the next twelve months, which was numbing but also exhilarating; Richard finally had found something that brought him enjoyment and, at the same time, challenged him.

During the first year, Richard was involved in or witnessed a dizzying array of human injuries and diseases: gunshot wounds to the face; acid burns; fractured mandibles, midfaces, and orbital rims; zygomatic and frontal sinus injuries; life-threatening head and neck infections; dental infections; benign and malignant lesions; congenital facial deformities; acquired deformities; and more. Basically, he witnessed man's inhumanity to his fellow man. It was as if the knife and gun clubs met every weekend to duke it out, resulting in terrible injuries. Instead of treating fellow citizens kindly and with respect, people were hell-bent on getting involved in other people's lives. "If you are minding your own business, you won't have time to be minding mine" seemed to be a decent creed to follow.

All the specialties had their particular burdens to shoulder.

The overworked, overwrought brotherhood of doctors, nurses, and technicians came together to share those burdens. To survive this baptism by fire, one had to be smart, agile, and improvisational; it was as if one were drinking from a fire hose.

After surviving his first year, Richard moved into the second year, which mainly consisted of didactic lectures and off-service rotations. The three- or four-month rotations included internal medicine, general surgery, anesthesiology, neurosurgery, and head and neck cancer surgery at M. D. Anderson Hospital. The off-service resident functioned as if he were a first-year resident in that particular specialty, so while on the general surgery rotation, Richard was treated as if he were a first-year general surgery resident. Things the upper-level residents did not particularly want to do fell to the first-year residents, including amputations, hemorrhoidectomies, wound debridement, and wound care. Many times, they just wanted a warm body to retract while they operated. An incredible amount of learning occurred during the second year. Two examples stood out: one concerning general medicine and one concerning general surgery.

While rotating on medicine, Richard was given much responsibility, including drug overdoses; retention of fluids, as in ascites; and diabetic management, to name just a few. He saw the effects of a sixteen-year-old who had injected peanut butter into his vein and a young woman who thought injecting horse urine intravenously would be a good idea. One middle-aged woman Richard was caring for, who had terminal breast cancer, died one night. Richard liked the woman, and hearing the news the next morning was just too much to bear. He left her empty room and found a quiet place to cry. Every day revealed the fallenness of mankind, and at times, it would overwhelm. He started becoming aware of the brevity of life; it truly was a wisp of smoke that was quickly extinguished. *We are here for such a short time. How shall we be remembered? Just another selfish one on life's run, a name unknown, unsung.*

One event on general surgery was a humiliating hemorrhoidectomy. While on the service one morning, Richard was given the assignment of lead surgeon in the removal of internal hemorrhoids, a procedure Richard knew nothing about. He'd never even seen an internal hemorrhoid. Not able to get out of the assignment, he raced to the surgery library—there was no internet or Google to consult at the time, of course—and quickly read about the technique of the surgery. Entering the operating theater with tachycardia and some nausea, he leaned heavily on the experiences of the surgical nurse and technicians. The nurse coached the fearful, quaking hemorrhoid surgeon each step of the way as the offending varicosities were identified. Because the vital cinch suture, which was crucial, had been placed too shallow, upon cutting, there was an immediate torrent of bright red blood issuing from the poor patient's rectum. Packing the area with tampons and all manner of stuffing did little to staunch the rivulet of blood. An SOS went out to the senior resident. The likeable redheaded fourth-year resident hailing from Arkansas appeared. He had the situation under control in moments. He spent the remainder of his time giving Richard a needed lecture on incompetence and his various other notable shortcomings.

In Richard's personal life, that was the time when he married Carolyn, and they set up housekeeping in a quiet old suburb of Houston. Also at the time, Richard met Karen, who had married a fellow resident. Their friendship lasted more than forty-five years as Karen became more like a sister to Richard. She developed into a dear friend, totally earning Richard's trust and respect. Richard felt a person was blessed if he or she had one to three people who carried the title of *friend*, and Karen was one who bore that moniker.

By the third and fourth years, the residents were back on their service, functioning as junior or senior residents. Each month, one was given more responsibilities, until, by the time of one's attaining chief resident status, there were twelve residents answering to him or her. The senior resident answered to the attending faculty, with all others answering either to the faculty or to the senior resident. It was usually residents teaching residents, with minimal faculty input. The adage "See one, do one, teach one" was followed. It was an efficient but flawed method fraught with potential errors, as evidenced by the botched hemorrhoidectomy.

Richard had cataloged a vast number of experiences by age thirty, but nothing to that point equaled or paralleled the birth of his first child, a little baby named Joshua Rice Patterson, his first of two sons. This was a complete paradigm shift, another Ebenezer, a marker in his life. Richard experienced agape love for the first time. This was not id or Eros but pure, sacrificial love. He was out of his mind with joy, which thrust him into hyperactive protection. Unknowingly, Richard had sown seeds of destruction with this adoration. As noted previously, he was a cultural, carnal Christian who was not well anchored in scripture and never mentored by a godly man, so of course, he got many things backward, one of which was making Joshua the center of creation at the expense of God, then wife, and then children. This appears to be a common occurrence today in America, where moms and dads almost deify their children. This is not God's order. We should worship God first; care for our spouse second; and then teach, love, protect, and discipline the children third.

During the residency program, Richard developed a close relationship with fellow resident David Haverkorn. Their friendship blossomed to the point where each viewed the other as the brother he'd never had. David was talented at building things, such as houses, furniture, a campfire, or an emergency outdoor shelter. He was a consummate outdoorsman and adept at fishing, hunting, guiding, and all-around surviving. Richard had rudimentary skills and knowledge concerning all things in which his friend was an expert. They bonded deeply, becoming best friends who believed they would grow old together, even skiing as old men, as they had done as young men. They shared a deep love and admiration. Nothing could have prepared Richard for the future dissolution of this cherished friendship.

Graduating from the residency program, in possession of a newly bestowed master of science degree for research he had published and a certificate of attainment for the requirements of an oral and maxillofacial surgeon, Richard now faced the daunting reality of providing for his family. Unsure of where to live, he decided to associate with a practice in Baytown, Texas.

It was a good decision, granting him stability and time to enjoy his life somewhat. It was almost an idyllic interlude before he had to make the hard choice of where to finally settle to raise the family. He pushed back against enormous pressure from his mother urging him to move back to California and come under the soothing ministrations and direction of the maternal umbrella. Mother was a strong-willed person who had overcome a terrible childhood, and she felt it best to have her family close under her benevolent direction. His sisters and their husbands succumbed to her siren song of encouragement, but Richard continued to resist. Something deep down and innate in his soul that he could not quite put his finger on told him that would not be a good idea. Time would prove him correct.

Due to a confluence of events and decisions, in 1979, Richard, with his small family in tow, settled in Plano, Texas, a rapidly growing suburb of Dallas. Obtaining a loan of $136,000 with an exorbitant interest rate of 22 percent, he prepared an office for his new practice. He hired three people and then waited for people to call for an appointment. He had sold the yellow Porsche, making enough money to place a down payment on a small home.

This was the time of President Jimmy Carter and all his failed Democratic policies, which resulted in gas shortages and high interest rates—a time of stagflation. Of course, an entire book could be written on the failed policies of the Democratic Party, from its racist inception, championing of the South during the Civil War, resistance to reconstruction, advocation of Jim Crow laws, and founding of the Ku Klux Klan to the present, where it is indistinguishable from socialism.

With the election of President Ronald Reagan, one of Richard's few heroes, a palpable sense of hope came over the nation.

In a short while, his second son was born, in 1980. Since Richard was so crazy about Joshua, he felt a little sorry for Jared; he was certain he had expended all his paternal love on Josh. But when seeing Jared Richard Patterson for the first time, he was amazed there was an untapped wellspring of love still for his beautiful second son. What utter joy it was as he bonded with this little bright-eyed, happy, active, and lovable boy. Jared had a sense of wonderment about him; everyone was attracted and drawn to him. Even when Jared was a child in elementary and middle school, the boys in his class wanted to know what kind of clothes or haircut Jared was sporting for that particular school year. He was a natural leader.

The boys were seldom left with or cared for by babysitters, with the exception of the grandparents. Since the grandparents lived at a distance in California and Houston, they were seldom availed upon. However, it was okay, as all settled into a rhythm and routine. Richard, fearful of not being able to provide for his family, worked long hours and was on the medical staff of fourteen hospitals, which kept him busy with emergencies and consults. As the practice became busier, he started eliminating appointments to all but three.

In his third year of practice, he hired an associate who was well trained and energetic, who became a full partner after twelve months. They managed to maintain a partnership for thirteen years and today remain friends.

Over the next ten years, they settled into a middle-class suburban routine: sports for the kids, a larger home, vacations, and school. They did life together with close friends and family. The boys were good athletes and competed in all the sports except football. Richard was involved in coaching baseball and basketball.

While coaching one game, Richard caught a hard-hit foul baseball in his left eye. Immediately diagnosing a blowout fracture, he drove himself to the hospital, where he was met by his surgical nurse and his practice partner. The nurse, his partner, and the emergency room physician all suggested immediate surgery. Richard, after reviewing the radiographs, decided against that treatment, opting instead to do nothing. Even the laceration under his eye was repaired using only Steri-Strips and not conventional sutures. Richard's philosophy was "Surgery is for doing, not having." This philosophy held firm even with a badly fractured collarbone sustained while showing off by jumping a bike from a steep ramp and with a wrist fractured while skiing. Orthopedic surgeon friends of Richard recommended surgery to repair the fractures, but Richard did not waver from his philosophy.

Much time and attention were given to select soccer, which was coached by a charismatic Iranian ex-national team player. Traveling to different tournament venues in Texas and Colorado, the family was in constant contact with this man, who had quite an attraction on all. Richard, managing a vibrant practice, with its attendant daily dramas at work, started investing less time in the relationships at home. He was naive and in denial of the little foxes ruining his vineyard. Sensing on a deep level something was not right, he struggled to understand the unraveling of his marriage. Each day was a major challenge.

One must remember the seas most people swam in during the turbulent 1960s, '70s, and '80s. God was being studied and relegated to a lesser position in one's life. We had all bought into the lie of progressive enlightenment: man had all the answers in this man-centric universe. Richard was not well anchored spiritually to withstand the coming gale. Arriving home each day from work, he was greeted with spousal distancing and a confusing atmosphere. This went on for more than a year, and even with the benefit of psychological counseling, which involved copious amounts of psychosocial babble, the marriage went into a fatal tailspin. After fourteen years of marriage, a divorce was filed, which was granted by the court.

Richard thought marriage was forever; but no-contest, easy divorce was the vogue of the day. No more hard work on relationships or compromise was needed in modern culture. The virtues of past generations were viewed as quaint and out of style. If one failed in any way in fulfilling his or her spouse's desires and make-believe fantasies, then one simply divorced. A generation or two of being influenced by doctors Spock, Masters, and Johnson; being encouraged to find oneself; and falsely believing that one deserved to be happy, among many other false narratives, resulted in frustrated people and failed relationships. The venomous seeds of free love and "Do your own thing" that had been planted were now germinating and sprouting. Society had once again bought into the lie of "Eat of this, and you too will be like God." The bottom line was, Richard was faced with a failed marriage and the responsibility of raising two young children—not uncommon or unusual for the 1970s to the present. We, as a nation, have made a mockery of the sacred marriage vows, pulling asunder all that God has joined.

A marriage ending in divorce involving children is like a never-healing wound; it is always open and raw. Of course, if there is abuse of any kind, divorce might be the best option.

The next ten years were tumultuous, with all affected persons going off the rails. Richard's wife moved out of the home, pursuing her own life, while Richard remained in the house with his two sons, trying to navigate this new, unwanted paradigm shift. It was sad to see the dissolution of a relationship, with everyone trying to find his or her footing. Many mistakes were made as hopes and dreams were shattered. Richard and his ex-wife became unintentionally adversarial in regard to the subject of the children. Richard basically took on the role of omniparent, driving the kids to school and sports activities, overseeing homework, cooking, doing laundry, cleaning house, managing a medical practice, and doing sundry other chores and tasks. This mandated a full day, allowing for little sleep, and, of course, was not an ideal situation. It started taking a toll on all.

The first child to start wobbling and eventually rebel against all the dysfunction was Joshua. His was an amazing story, and God clearly was working in the mess of it all. The home morphed into a meeting place and hostel for both boys' friends who were escaping their own dysfunctional messes. Many a morning, upon awakening, Richard would discover that one to three of the boys had slept over and were now hungry, needing to be fed. The go-to quick breakfast usually involved Whataburger breakfast burritos. Richard always tried to cook the evening meal, which included a rotating menu of five meals that took no more than thirty minutes' cooking time. The hectic pace began taking a toll on Richard. He began to enlist housekeepers to help ease the load, but it turned out they were more of a problem than help. One, who was a live-in housekeeper, turned out to be a bona fide witch. The boys reported to Richard they had discovered her reciting ritual incantations late one night in her room. Of course, she was let go, but she had brought evil into the home. Many years later, in a yearlong study of evil and demons, Richard came to realize what a profoundly negative impact the drama had on his family.

The consequences of the divorce began to really manifest in Josh. The once bright, energetic, joyful boy started to withdraw from family and seek his own way. He became rebellious, seeking guidance and wisdom from the world. The world was willing and able to lead the young man astray. Whoever tells the best story usually wins, and the world was telling the best story at the time. At least Josh believed so. Richard, in a panic, tried harder to be his friend and be a cool, indulgent father instead of doing the harder work of setting boundaries and being a disciplinarian. The boys were crying out for structure in their confusing world, but Richard was not a healthy father. Instead, he followed the windy emanations of the secular so-called experts. Somewhat similar to King David, as told in 2 Samuel of the Bible, Richard was a poor, indulgent father. His loose attitude toward discipline was a contributing factor in his sons' sins and failures. The sad results were two sons and a father who were totally dysfunctional.

After spending more than $100,000 on psychological counseling, rehabilitation centers, and special schools for troubled children, the Patterson family were still in crisis mode. However, the efforts were lifesaving for the boys, as they bought time.

But not all was misery. During these single years, Richard indulged himself on trips to Mexico or the Caribbean islands, pursuing pleasure. He and the boys learned scuba diving, enjoying it immensely.

Richard was not a good swimmer and had a healthy fear of water, which had developed at an early age. However, one did not need to be a good swimmer to dive, and with instructions, he learned how to scuba. Many times, he traveled with his good friend Dick McFarland on these trips. Richard listened and learned from people who had dived all over the world, who recounted tales of danger and death. While having drinks one night, two French divers told of underwater waterfalls and how they'd managed to escape after being caught in one while in the Red Sea. This tidbit of information was helpful on a dive when Richard was caught in a waterfall while observing a reef face at one hundred feet. Paired with Dick and a dive master, Richard found himself tumbling down and away from the other two due to a waterfall, until he lost sight of them. Alone and fighting against panic and a malfunctioning dive computer, he finally surfaced, finding no boats in sight. After about twenty minutes, a boat came by, picked him up, and delivered him to his boat. He waited until finally Dick and the master surfaced, out of air, thinking Richard had drowned. After a short history of about twenty-five dives, Richard was finished. He felt there was no sense in tempting fate anymore concerning immersing himself in water. Operating on terra firma was dangerous enough.

During that time, Richard and the boys learned to ski, with the sons on snowboards and Dad on skis. They experienced a number of fun times in Colorado, New Mexico, and Utah. Richard was also starting to date, and he had two somewhat serious relationships. Since he was psychologically unhealthy, he, of course, chose women who themselves had issues. There were many red flags raised by his sons, friends, and family members concerning the women, but Richard glibly overlooked all concerns and proffered advice. His dear friends Karen, Dick, the Haverkorns, and others could not persuade him of the obvious pitfalls. The women fulfilled his many selfish needs, the greatest being escapism. They were fun and encouraged him to concentrate on himself at the expense of all others, including his children. Obviously, this was poor advice and a terrible mistake. Richard spent many years ruing and repenting of this horrid sin.

But again, God was working in the mess.

CHAPTER 14

Dad Dying and Miracles

A few consequential events happened while Richard was stuck in the muck and mire of his life. He had taken a number of medical missionary trips to Mexico and Guatemala. On the outings, he noticed that most of the doctors, pilots, and other volunteers were Christian. He did not realize at the time that the seed of the gospel of Jesus Christ was being nurtured in his soul, and his life would make a dramatic pivot as this seed started to bear fruit.

On one such trip, he traveled with both sons to northern Mexico. The area was a hotbed of witchcraft. Rolando, an ex-lumberjack from Oregon, and his wife had planted a church there many years before. They were well received by the locals, and the little church compound thrived; it was always open, inviting all to enter. Rolando constantly gave bags of rice or beans to the hungry people as they came to the little compound. Richard visited the area many times, and each time, he witnessed people coming and going and worshipping, with many spending the night, sleeping on the roof of the little church. Many local pastors, having been trained by Rolando, were there helping over a three-day period as many hundreds of poor were treated. It was always exhausting work but also incredibly satisfying.

At the end of day three on one of the mission trips, while eating dinner at the pastor's small home, Richard overheard them talking matter-of-factly about a miracle that had happened about two weeks prior. It was surreal, almost as if they were just talking about the weather. A young boy of four had died early one morning, and the grieving parents, in desperation, spent most of the day going from one witch to another, who cast magic spells in an effort to resuscitate the boy. Of course, none of the entreaties worked. In the evening, they brought their dead son to Pastor Rolando, asking for help. Rolando was rough around the edges but a righteous man of God. These people lived with death and knew what it looked like—different from the sanitized version of most Americans. He replied to their request, "All we can do is pray," as they carried the body into the church. With many of the small flock of believers praying and laying hands on the body, God decided to show out at that moment. God vivified and raised the small dead body to life, much as He had done for His friend Lazarus two thousand years before.

Of course, Richard was shocked upon hearing this and was disinclined to believe it had actually happened. But they were all sitting around talking about the event much as one would have discussed any trivial matter. Richard, being trained in the sciences, had great difficulty in believing this had happened. But it was a teachable moment God used in Richard's walk of sanctification.

About three weeks later, driving home from work, Richard was questioning the veracity of the supposed resurrection miracle, when God spoke to the doubting Thomas. Richard was stunned as he sat in traffic and heard the God of all creation rebuke and upbraid him. There was no discussion or dialogue, just God speaking: "I dare you question me and my deeds. I don't need your understanding or approval to do what I do. I indeed raised the boy, and the only thing you need to do is worship me." Richard was thunderstruck at the revelation and the interaction. It had a profound effect on all that happened going forward. Richard witnessed many occurrences of miracles, some large, such as that one, and some small, such as healings. His constant prayer became "God, help my unbelief." There were a number of missionary trips to orphanages, villages, and small churches over a period of many years, each impacting his life. Also impacting his life and others in the family was the dying of his father.

The passing of the patriarch unfolded in stages. It was a grace of God, allowing each family member time to adjust to the reality that Grampers was no more. During those times, God showed up in a big way, strengthening faith and preparing hearts to bid him farewell. The first occasion happened when Richard was away at school in Tennessee, and Dad experienced a heart attack. Mom took him to the emergency room at two o'clock in the morning with chest pains, and the doctor in the small hospital assured her that it appeared he was experiencing indigestion and not a cardiac event. While he was speaking with her, another patient, who was being treated for a hand laceration, rushed out of the room and told the startled doctor that it appeared the man with indigestion had just died. Quickly performing CPR and cardioverting his heart, the doctor was able to revive him. After cardiac bypass surgery and recovery, Dad was back to normal.

Many years later, Richard asked his father if he remembered the event. Richard was shocked as his rough-hewn father retold in great detail about leaving his body. As he arose above his lifeless form, beckoned by Jesus in white robes, Dad felt a sense of overpowering joy. He was ecstatic. Then he was suddenly angry as his heart was shocked back to life, and that Goodness was suddenly taken from him. The story, shared only once with Richard, was amazing because it involved his father, who did not often speak of spiritual things.

The second experience involved Richard and his two boys witnessing Grampers dying in his battle with Legionnaires' disease. As his health rapidly deteriorated, the doctors were able to keep him alive until Richard and his sons could travel from Texas to his bedside. Upon arriving on a Saturday morning, all three entered his hospital room to an alert man. Excited to see the three, Grampers started visiting, but three times, he stopped midsentence. The first time, he asked Jared, who was standing next to Richard, "Do you see that man at the foot of the bed?"

Since no one was standing there, Jared smiled and said, "No, Grampers, I don't see him."

Grampers responded, "That's interesting. Josh, do you see that man sitting on the monitors next to you?"

"No, I don't, Grampers," answered Josh.

Then Grampers said, "Well, that beats everything; there are men standing throughout the room."

It appeared he was seeing angels who were not visible to Richard or the boys. He made a miraculous recovery and was discharged the next day. This brief interaction of the natural and the supernatural was eerie and thought-provoking for Richard.

There were a few more supernatural events concerning the premature departure of Richard's dad. About five years after the angel incident, seven family members were present at his deathbed. He was in the process of dying, lying in bed, alert and talking. From about one in the morning until daybreak, no doctors or nurses came into the room, which was unusual. Dad was inclined in bed, performing rowing movements with his arms. Richard's sister

Shirley, sitting next to him, asked what he was doing. He replied he was in a boat, rowing to a shore where a beautiful man in white awaited him. He said, "I can't quite get there."

Shirley quietly suggested, "Dad, just relax and sleep."

That was what he did. No one else spoke; it seemed as if there were an aura of holiness about the room, as if all were in the presence of angels. The indescribable feeling and silence lasted from about two o'clock till five o'clock in the morning, when a nurse finally entered the room. Upon the taking of his vital signs, he awoke, saying, "Boy, that sure was interesting last night, wasn't it? I am ready to go home."

He was indeed discharged that same morning to the surprise of all, including his doctors. The Lord would give the family another five years with Dad before he peacefully died at home with Sue and Mom holding his wizened, withered hands as he murmured and spoke softly with the attending angels. God strengthened the family's faith and understanding in the last twenty years of Dad's life.

Life at home was becoming more chaotic and unmanageable. It seemed no amount of effort or prayer made much of a difference in the trajectories of the boys' or Richard's lives. Joshua became more rebellious, distancing himself from the family. Josh was trying to find his footing and purpose but was floundering. Richard was not attending church, so the boys were not exposed to that possible healing balm. However, Josh was invited to a church camp by some friends, which turned out to be life-changing for him and for Richard.

Of course, God orchestrated the entire event; He was after Josh like a hound out of heaven. The church organizing the camp retreat was large and prestigious. Soon upon arrival at the camp,

Josh was found with contraband materials that were verboten, such as cigarettes and other inappropriate items. A decision had to be made: send him home or confiscate the materials and let him stay. Intriguingly, Josh's future father-in-law was the pastor who made the decision to let him stay at camp for the remainder of the week. This was life-changing for Josh, demonstrating much grace and wisdom on the part of the pastor. Another man who was influential in mentoring Josh and introducing him to the gospel of Jesus Christ was also involved in the decision.

As Josh was battling his demons and stumbling forward, his little brother, Jared, was watching and taking it all in. "Little brothers often see what older brothers do, the good, the bad, the ugly, things they will rue"—this line of poetry pretty well sums up what happened to Jared. Of course, it was more complicated than that, but still, he lurched from one crisis to another, seemingly helpless to staunch the bleeding destruction enveloping his life.

That period in Richard's life took on nightmarish proportions. No amount of effort, money, or therapy directed at the slowly unfolding train wreck helped. The never-healing wound of the divorce extracted its heavy toll on sweet-spirited Jared. Twenty-eight years passed before this prodigal son regained his footing and came home. God is good, and His timing is perfect, but the journey can be painful and confusing. Thousands of prayers ascended to God, begging Him for deliverance of this son. God heard and responded. The lesson here is this: never give up on a child and tire, but be long-suffering, obedient, and diligent in trusting the Lord. We can only find true joy in Him as He is glorified.

CHAPTER 15

Sons

Richard continued to battle his demons with his own feeble strength, all the while becoming more desperate. He was chasing after his own demigods and idols. Lust, money, and acceptance by others were just a few on his long laundry list of idols. John Calvin, the great Reformer theologian, famously stated, "The human heart is an idol factory," and if we are honest, we know it to be true. People elevate things that are good and necessary to a position displacing God from the center of their attention. But God was working in the mess that was Richard's life. A number of central events happened during that time, and two of the three involved Joshua.

One Saturday night, at about one o'clock in the morning, Richard received a telephone call from the hospital emergency room physician, informing him that his son Joshua had sustained a fractured lower jaw in two places. Thinking it was just another call in a long line of late-night calls concerning Josh, Richard asked to speak to his son. She put Josh on the phone, and he informed his dad that he and some buddies had been in a brawl, resulting in the fractured jaw. Arriving at the emergency room, Richard was greeted by a dejected, remorseful Josh, who kept apologizing and asking for forgiveness—an unexpected response from the rebellious young man. He kept telling his father how much he loathed himself at that moment. He felt unclean and unworthy—a posture Jesus understands and always welcomes. It was surreal as Richard operated on his own son early in the morning, repairing the fractures. He had an overwhelming sense of love and protection for his son in that moment. It was as if he were being birthed anew at that moment. Every sense was on high alert; Daddy was there, and he was going to protect and nurse his child back to health. But doubt still resonated in Richard's mind, as he had been disappointed before in new beginnings concerning Josh.

Making rounds the next morning at eleven, Richard came to Josh's room, which was filled with his running buddies, who told him he had to get well soon so they could travel to Austin in a week, where they had rented an apartment in anticipation of attending junior college. As Richard was writing discharge orders, he was also listening to the excited conversation concerning living away from home and attending college. Richard could hardly believe what he heard next as Josh informed his friends they would have to go without him, as he was staying home with his dad to attend junior college locally. It was a 180-degree turn in Joshua's life, marking a monumental shift.

The next year was one of the most memorable of Richard's life. He and his son started repairing and mending their relationship and strengthening the bond between them. Joshua became a new man as he underwent mentoring by Tom Bailey, one of the men involved in the decision to let Josh stay at the church camp years before. After his first year of junior college, Josh decided to transfer to Utah State College. He eventually graduated from Texas A&M University. He was one of the few Richard ever witnessed with a true Damascus Road experience. Much like the apostle Paul, Josh was lost one moment, and the next moment, he was found. Joshua never looked back or wavered; he went forward and was profoundly influential in shaping many people's lives.

During that period, Josh met Natalie, his future wife, who was the daughter of the pastor who'd discovered Josh's contraband at the church camp. Only God could have orchestrated this sequence of events. Josh, with trepidation, approached Neil, the pastor, to ask permission to date his precious daughter. It could have been one of Neil's worst fears, but to his great credit, he realized Josh was a changed man. Wisely, he gave permission for Josh to date his daughter but with a few caveats, with one being that he had to come to Neil's office every three months to give him the state of the union on the dating activities. This Josh did faithfully for seven years before marrying Natalie. The ceremony, officiated by Neil, was witnessed by about six hundred people.

Their union produced four unbelievable grandchildren. The dating and courtship of Nat and Josh were an example to many. Following God's plan just seems to work out the best.

Josh's younger brother, Jared, continued to struggle mightily, drifting further from family. Every corrective measure failed. Sweet Jared desperately tried to adjust and find any stable ground to stand upon. His father, in a perpetual panic, tried to rescue his flailing son. The emotional pain was horrible and relentless, affecting all aspects of Richard's life. There was a sense that nothing would ever be normal. The more Richard tried to rescue Jared, the further away he drifted. The entire melodramatic play was insane; Richard tried everything, with no stone left unturned, but the results were always the same.

CHAPTER 16

Epiphanies

Josh was now on the right path, but Jared was struggling on the wrong path, and Richard was exhausted and out of options after years of failing. While Richard was driving home from work one day, the second of three events occurred. The first had involved Josh's spiritual epiphany, and this one involved Richard, as he had run out of ideas and hope. For the second time in his life, there was again a tangible presence of God inside the car with him. This time, Richard was wailing more than crying while shaking his puny fist at the Creator of the universe. Challenging God out of desperation, he started ranting. "I give up! If you are so wonderful and powerful, you take this mess, and fix it. I am finished!" Richard was angry and scared. The rant went on for a few minutes, with intermittent crying, wailing, and various gesticulations. Fellow motorists at the stoplights surely wondered what was going on inside that car.

As emotions were spent and lamentations were exhausted, the inside of the car became as quiet as a sanctuary, and the air had holiness about it. God spoke. As before, He spoke quietly but plainly to Richard, reassuring him: "I have this. Just trust me. I love Jared more than you love him." A great peace fell upon Richard. Really for the first time, Richard believed God was working in the middle of this man-made catastrophe. Things that previously had been blurry started coming into clearer focus.

God had once again gotten Richard's attention, and his life started to change. Jared's life was still out of control, but Richard's was coming under control.

The third event once again involved Joshua. One evening, at about ten o'clock, Richard was winding down, thinking about bed, when Josh entered the living room, wanting to know if they could talk. Richard had always encouraged both boys to come to him to talk about anything. Thinking Josh wanted to share something concerning himself or maybe ask for sage wisdom or guidance from his dad, Richard was shocked and taken aback when Josh said, "Dad, this is very difficult for me to say, but do you know why your life is a mess and your relationships with women do not work out?"

Richard thought, *How dare you speak to your father like that! First of all, it's none of your business! I should be giving you advice, not you giving your fifty-year-old father advice. What kind of wisdom could a twenty-year-old impart to a now upset parent?*

With unbelievable grace and humility, Josh said, "Dad, God is not honoring your relationships because you are not honoring God in the way you relate to women." Then he went on to say, "I have made a vow to God and myself to remain chaste until marriage. Can you?"

Richard was struck to his core because all the things said were true. The words convicted Richard of his many sins. Josh was correct in his penetrating diagnostics. With his pride damaged by the gentle rebuke, Richard, through clenched teeth, spat out his acceptance of the challenge. Josh told his dad he loved him and went to bed as Richard plotted his strategy.

CHAPTER 17

Janie

Joshua and others could see that Richard had undergone a profound change trending toward psychological healing. However, healthy mental health was a slow, painful work in progress, requiring another twenty years of often difficult, heartbreaking effort. It was hard to undo years of stinking thinking overlaid with poor decision-making. Twenty years of difficult pruning was required.

Josh again took initiative, approaching his father now as matchmaker. Through his network of friends, he had discovered the name of a potential blind date for his dad. The lady reportedly attended the same church Richard occasionally attended. She had a sterling reputation and was the same age as Richard, which was unusual, as he normally dated younger women. Her name was Janie, and she was a successful businesswoman and had been single for many years, raising her only child, a son named Troy. Richard had been a single parent for a number of years and was still in the process of actively parenting. Josh kept up a steady two-month drumbeat mantra of "Do you want to see if I can get her number so you can at least call her?"

Finally, after months of persistent asking, Richard relented, saying, "Yes, give me her number," thinking it would end the nagging.

Janie had never met Richard and had not dated in years. She

91

was successful in her work and spent much time doing life together with her many friends in the small group at church. She had been involved with this group of friends for more than twenty years, and they were influential in mentoring her. Being the only single lady in the group, she was mildly frustrated about not being married. Janie confided in an older, wiser woman about this, and the advice the woman gave included making a list of ten things Janie desired in a mate. Then she was to pray about seeing what God might do: if she brought more glory to God by remaining single, then so be it; however, if she brought glory to Him by marrying, then so be it.

Taking the lady's advice became the backstory for what happened next. A friend of Janie's knew a friend who knew Richard, so she was expecting an ensuing telephone call. Of course, this was all unknown to Richard at the time.

Wanting to get his son off his back, Richard finally called Janie. Really not wanting to date, Richard did not open the conversation with pleasantries but with a "Hello, Janie. This is Richard Patterson, and I am supposed to call you so we can meet."

She said, "Yes, I was expecting your call, but I am going to be out of town for the next two weeks."

Elated at hearing this, he was ready to hang up, when she said, "But I can meet with you when I return."

Quickly calculating that this was not going to be as easy as he'd thought, he set a lunch date for a Thursday so he might quickly exit after a brief lunch.

When the day arrived, Richard, being early, was sitting at a table, when in walked a beautiful, stunning, well-dressed lady. She walked up, introducing herself. Richard was shocked at her beauty, carriage, and mannerisms. The brief lunch morphed into an almost two-hour introduction. Pheromones, it seemed, were in the air.

As lunch came to a close, Janie said, "I am sure you need to get back to work."

Since Richard usually did not work on Thursdays, he said, "No, there is no rush."

Janie, having no idea of Richard's employment, later told her friends, "Well, this is rich. This interesting man doesn't even have a job."

Walking her to her car, Richard found himself asking her for a date the following evening. As soon as the words were out of his mouth, cool Richard could not believe what he had just said. He sounded like a desperate man—which was entirely true. She accepted.

The next evening, he arrived to pick her up for a movie. Entering her home, he was met by Janie's longtime friend Kathy. Hours of visiting came and went. The movie was forgotten. As Kathy left, she gave Janie two thumbs up on her find, reassuring her that Richard did not appear to be a knuckle-dragging ax murderer.

Richard, having a poor record in choosing women to date, now wanted to make sure he had made a good decision. He introduced Janie to his friends Karen and Dick McFarland for their assessment. As they sat outside on their back porch, imbibing adult beverages, the conversation was relaxed, flowing easily, with much laughter. Upon leaving, Richard received two thumbs up from his two dear friends. This was encouraging. He couldn't wait to show Janie off to other friends and family, especially his two sons. Everyone adored her, and Richard thanked God for his good fortune. He also told himself, *For once in your miserable life, don't mess this up.*

Both were obviously attracted to each other. They started dating only each other, and on the fourth date, they had an interesting conversation. Richard, at the end of a wonderful evening attending the Van Cliburn piano competition in Fort Worth, informed Janie about his promise of chastity and said he was going to date and court her with honor. Janie informed Richard that was wonderful since that was also her intention. That took premarital intimacy off the table and immediately simplified dating going forward. Every time they were together, they talked and laughed, getting to know each other well, understanding that at the end of the evening, they were going their separate ways. Obviously, this was contrary to the prevailing wisdom of the day being championed. However, following the wisdom of the world was a big reason for Richard's failed relationships with women in the first place. He had made a vow to God and his son to follow the Bible's pattern in dating, courtship, and eventual marriage.

It was an awesome, intense, fun, short courtship. In a mere three months, Richard, on bended knee in a private room in an upscale restaurant at eleven at night, asked Janie to marry him by way of a poem he had written for the occasion. She answered yes, setting Richard's heart aflutter. He had for sure outpunted his coverage.

They were married on November 8, 1997, a short three months after the proposal. Janie planned the entire ceremony, inviting about one hundred guests. As the pianist played Mendelssohn's "Wedding March," the couple almost ran to the altar and awkwardly waited for the frustrated pianist to improvise an ending. When asked, "Who gives this woman in marriage?" all the men in Janie's longtime home group from church stood in unison, declaring, "We do." It was a moving moment. Richard's friends from California and Janie's from the Midwest were in attendance, making the moment even more special. After the ceremony, they were off to a well-appointed reception but only stayed briefly; then they boarded a plane bound for Italy.

The honeymoon was fabulous; they had stars in their eyes at every venue visited. Janie and the love Richard had for her aged well. They remain totally and deeply in love with each other even to the present day at age seventy-five.

Janie brought more than herself to the marriage; she also brought new relationships: Helen, Nancy, and Troy. Helen, Janie's mom, was a pleasant lady who always sided with the sons-in-law, sometimes to the frustration of her daughters. She was a wonderful cook well known for her pies with crusts so light they seemed to almost float. She and a group of friends met at least once a week for coffee and pie for seventy years. She and her friends lived long lives; the youngest died in her nineties, and a few passed the century mark. It has been good-naturedly said that there must be something in the water of Coon Rapids, Iowa (the fabled fountain of youth of Ponce de Leon?).

Janie had a wonderful older sister, Nancy, who had been the one to name Janie. At eight years old, she longed for a little sister, so when her mother, Helen, became pregnant, she was elated. Currently reading the book *Dick and Jane*, she chose the name Jane for her new sister. Janie and Nancy had a great relationship and were the best of sisters, always chatting and laughing as if they had not spoken in ages. Many things were charming about Nancy, but an enduring characteristic was not taking herself too seriously. Nancy had a certain bon vivant air about her, earning her the moniker Fancy Nancy. She could easily have been a flapper girl in the Roaring Twenties or a high-fashion designer in any era. She was a large personality in a small midwestern town. Such is life: "The best-laid plans of mice and men often go astray." Everyone loved being around Fancy Nancy. She remains energetic and vivacious at age eighty-three.

Richard met Troy, Janie's son, early in their relationship. Troy was likeable and easy to be around. When Janie and Richard married, Richard viewed Troy more as a son than a stepson. His father had abandoned both wife and son when Troy was about three years old, so he'd grown up without a father figure; however, he spent many summers in Coon Rapids, where Nancy and John assumed surrogate parental responsibilities. Troy was a friend almost to a fault; he would give a person the shirt off his back and, much like Jared, would defend all against bullies. Troy was also a great impersonator, giving great imitations of various characters. He married Cathi, a pretty woman whom everyone liked, but she remained reserved and was not well known by many. Richard came to really get to know and like her as she and he drove thirteen hours to Coon Rapids, Iowa, for Janie's mom's funeral. They talked nonstop, losing track of time and almost running out of gas once, finding themselves a hundred miles out of the way in Cedar Rapids, Iowa. Some good came from the mistake: racing through the backcountry farm roads of Iowa and seeing parts of the country previously unseen by them.

It was a sad day when Cathi, at age forty-six, passed away in Richard and Janie's home from cervical cancer.

CHAPTER 18

---ᘛᘚ---

Routines

Arriving home from Italy, Richard and Janie settled into a routine. Both worked. Janie had a wonderful job in sales. Richard's boys both lived at home, but Josh was usually away at school. Janie's son, Troy, lived on his own until marrying Cathi about a year after Richard and Janie's wedding. Joshua was studying premed while attending Texas A&M University. Dear Jared was still struggling.

Janie was made of different stuff than most people were, as evidenced by traits of long-suffering and great compassion seasoned with wonderful wisdom. She was always supportive of Richard and his sometimes poorly thought-out decisions. The challenges were never financial but revolved around the children. The new family blended well, but Richard, trying to avoid confrontations, developed a keen art of enablement concerning his children.

This grievous error prolonged any semblance of normalcy concerning his boys. Richard felt sorry about the divorce, trying his best to lessen the impact by indulging his sons and being a best friend instead of a healthy father. This sick thinking required years of patient instruction by Janie and others before Richard came to his senses. A terrible price was paid by all, especially the boys. There were much repentance and many offered prayers to God concerning this dysfunction. Spoiler alert: this narrative had a happy ending.

An interesting look inside Janie's heart early in the marriage came in the subject of tithing. As a single man, Richard usually gave about twenty to forty dollars, if he gave at all. However, Janie had been convicted years before meeting Richard to give consistently and more abundantly. Asking Richard one day about his habit of miserly giving, she received a weak answer as Richard changed the subject. She shared her concerns with a friend, and they both agreed they would pray to see if God might change Richard's heart.

This was all unknown to Richard. But one day, months after the onetime non-nagging conversation, God did change Richard's heart, convicting him to now tithe proportionately, as his wife suggested. When Richard brought this new revelation to Janie's attention, she started crying. Confused, Richard asked her what was wrong. Upon hearing her story, he was moved, realizing the gentle workings of God's heart in changing his heart by the tender ministrations of Janie's heart. She never nagged; she prayed.

In spite of challenges, their marriage was fun, including many trips taken with friends, an active social scene, wonderful dinners at trendy restaurants, and the coming together of blended families. God knew what He was doing by bringing Richard and Janie together. They melded perfectly, with the same quirks, passions, and shared extended family values. However, Janie came from a small town of one thousand in Iowa. Coon Rapids, Iowa, resembled somewhat of a Norman Rockwell painting depicting a small midwestern town. The town had an oversized history. Janie recalled Soviet Union president Nikita Khrushchev coming to her town with an American contingent, including Adlai Stevenson, to study the techniques of developing and planting hybrid-seed corn. At the time, Garst Seed Company was the largest hybrid-seed company in the world. Janie's school was excused for the day so the kids could line up on Main

Street to see and greet the president of the Soviet Union. There was a powerful adversary, now patting the top of Janie's head. Janie lived an unusual life in many ways; interesting things happened to and around her much like Forrest Gump in the movie.

One amazing story concerned an airplane crash with ensuing fire at the New Orleans airport when she was an airline attendant. While she was sleeping in her second-floor room after flying all day, a Delta training flight crashed into the hotel she was in, setting it ablaze. Shocked to wakefulness, Janie looked out the window at a greasy black-orange ball of fire. Rushing out the door to escape, she realized there was no obvious exit. Yelling for help, she heard a man's voice telling her to follow his instructions. She did, eventually finding a Mr. Evelsizer, who covered her with a blanket and drove her to the hospital. With her hair singed off, hands burned, and torso peeling, the doctors and nurses at first thought she was a black patient because of the oily dark residue covering her. Mr. Evelsizer told her to take off a ring her father had given her and give it to him since her hands were rapidly swelling. Janie did as instructed, as he told her he worked for Delta and had been on a smoke break when he witnessed the accident.

Eventually discharged, Janie traveled back to Coon Rapids, where she recovered with no scarring due to retired Dr. Johnson, who lived next door, and his daily ministrations. After about a month, an envelope arrived in the mail with her ring in it but with no note or return address, just the ring. Janie told her mother, Helen, she needed to call Delta to get the address for Mr. Evelsizer to thank him. However, Delta informed Janie they had never had anyone by that name working for the company, and besides, no one from Delta was working at that late hour.

It appeared the man never existed. The family believed it was a miracle and possibly an angel who rescued Janie that night. The wonderful, mysterious Mr. Evelsizer.

Many things happened to Janie, some good, some bad, and some hilarious. A good thing was when she was first-chair clarinetist at age fourteen when her little high school won first place in the Iowa school competition. A hilarious incident involved her chasing down her car as it rolled down the street in traffic, while wearing high heels. Flinging open the door, she was able to climb in and bring it to a stop before rolling into the four-way intersection. Of course, it was funny to her but terrifying to onlookers.

She was always in a hurry, which resulted in earrings caught in clothing often, clothing worn inside out, missing accessories, misplaced cell phone and keys, and the forgetting of this or that, all the while laughing at herself often and never taking herself too seriously. Spilled milk, exploding ketchup bottles, burned cookies, and clanging and banging around never upset her. She believed these little mishaps were no big deal, which endeared her to all. Honesty, sincerity, wisdom, and transparency were just a few of her wonderful attributes that made her lovable to her fortunate friends and family.

Richard and Janie had the opportunity to be involved in the Bill Glass prison ministry, making numerous trips inside various prisons to share the gospel of Christ. Richard's first outing was with the men in his home group at church. It was held at the Walls Unit at Huntsville State Prison, the place where Texas executed its prisoners. Richard was familiar with the place, as he had spent every Monday for a year there, treating prisoners, while he was a resident. But this three-day visit was different, as he would be sharing the gospel with as many inmates as possible. Richard was all fired up for the outing and was well read, fancying himself quite the theologian. He was ready to show off his knowledge and shower the men with wisdom, all gleaned from God, of course. However, God was having none of this nonsense and was ready to discipline and humble Richard.

It was a Thursday afternoon. Prep work and instructions were given before the eager evangelists were loosed upon the hapless inmates. The first prisoner God placed Richard in front of was a tattooed forty-five-year-old Mexican ex–gang banger standing behind two sets of bars adjacent to death row. The first thing to catch Richard's eye was the man's cot, on which lay a number of neatly underlined and annotated Bibles; in other words, these were well-used books. After a brief introduction, Richard learned of the man's difficult life. Speaking with him for a while, Richard got the sense that he was in the presence of a righteous, holy man. Richard was now being convicted of his presumption and condescension. The feelings of God's presence and Richard's sinfulness were overwhelming. Richard started weeping.

This brokenness of Richard continued for the next day and a half as this kind fellow brother in Christ continued ministering and teaching the ostensibly free man. Richard sat at the feet of this saint, never visiting another prisoner. He was completely broken and contrite; all his vaunted learning amounted to little as he was gently nurtured and taught by this humble brother in Christ. This man was never going to be released from prison, and he was at peace with that. His ministry was discipleship of other prisoners. The entire episode had a tremendous effect upon Richard's spiritual life going forward, as God humbled an arrogant Richard by using the "least of these."

Another experience concerning this ministry involved Janie and a men's prison in Oklahoma. The women were supposed to go into the women's prisons, but on this occasion, the warden was very anti-Christian and would not allow the women into the prison. However, with some manipulation and maneuvering, some were allowed into the men's prison. Janie volunteered to go, and soon she found herself surrounded by many hundreds of inmates in the middle of the prison yard. This beautiful lady was out of her element and becoming a bit unnerved, when all of a sudden, out of the crowd, a large man started advancing toward her. The other men began to melt back into the crowd, forming a perimeter, leaving only the two in the arena. He ordered two stools to be brought forward, on which they sat. The place became quiet as Janie began sharing the gospel with this prison boss, El Jefe. Janie spent thirty minutes with this man, feeling safe and, at the same time, praising God for the opportunity to share the Good News with him.

The last time Richard and Janie were involved in this ministry was in Dallas, where they spent a day at the girls' juvenile facility. It was unusual that Richard was allowed to go with Janie into that unit. They spent the day surrounded by girls aged ten to eighteen years of age. The young girls crowded around Richard, moving slowly next to him, with many touching him with affectionate, gentle touches. Richard was talking, the girls were listening, and the guards were observing.

As lunchtime came, Richard and Janie were leaving to eat, when the main guard approached Richard, telling him that she had been watching and that he should continue to love on the girls, as he had been doing. She said it was probably the first time any man had shown any attention to them in any normal way. All the girls, she informed Richard, had been sexually molested, usually by a stepfather, uncle, father, grandfather, or close friend. This broke Richard's heart.

In the afternoon, the girls just wanted to sit and talk. Upon his asking what their biggest disappointment was, almost all said it was losing their virginity in the way it had happened. That was when Richard told them the story in the book of Joel in the Bible wherein God says He will "restore to you … what the locust has eaten." They were excited to hear the story and started talking among themselves. Richard told them to pray that God would do this for them and give them peace.

CHAPTER 19

Friendship

Settling into a comfortable, routine life was good. Janie worked for a few years and then retired, while Richard continued his practice. The last five years, he practiced alone since his partnership had dissolved. Janie and Richard had a number of good friends, and they often traveled together on vacations. Trips to Italy, Mexico, Canada, and many places throughout the United States became sources of great memories.

People usually are lulled into a sense that a good thing just naturally continues, such as a great friendship. But as Richard aged, it became evident that a person was blessed indeed if he truly had one to three real friends. This fact was brought jarringly home when he lost a couple of dear friends' friendship over a seemingly innocuous event.

Janie and Richard and the couple traveled extensively together. They spent many weekends at each other's homes. Richard watched as their two beautiful children grew into successful adults. They were good kids, so he was astonished when one night, at about ten thirty, the son's wife showed up at Richard's door, sobbing. The young wife, the daughter-in-law of their friends, spent hours detailing the unfaithfulness of her husband. When she left to go home, Richard was determined to confront the young husband the next day, which he did. Having known the young man for more than twenty-five years, he started warning him about the pitfalls of unfaithfulness, eventually prevailing upon him to stop his actions and begin reconciling with his wife. With the benefit of wise counseling and the good work of the Lord, the marriage survived, producing five lovely daughters. Out of this sin, God changed their hearts, and they became marriage counselors in their church.

However, the incident had a bittersweet ending concerning Richard. His longtime friends were outraged that Richard and Janie had had the umbrage to interfere and confront their son over his sin. No amount of talking or explaining would change their minds, not even the fact that the young man and his wife had sought out the advice and help of the Pattersons. It was almost as if a person were ready to leap off a building, and they were not supposed to yell, "Stop! Don't jump!" Richard grieved the loss of the friendship for years, coming to realize God was weaning him away from investing too much hope in people at the expense of taking his eyes off God, the Perfecter of one's faith.

As he aged, Richard pondered much on the subject of friendship. In youth, many are deemed one's friend, but in the battering and travails of life, this larger group is winnowed to just a few. Even late in life, after much nurturing and time spent in developing a new friendship, it often turned out to be fool's gold; both Richard and the friend devolved into fair-weather friends.

After seventy-five years of life, he is blessed to count Dick and Karen McFarland; Bobby Jones; Janie; and his sisters, Sue and Shirley, as his stalwart, through-and-through friends who know him well. Others are fine acquaintances whom he admires and loves. However, they know little of Richard's fears, deep secrets, longings, stains, and blots; few people are invited into that arena. There is opportunity for new friends to enter late in life. All friends are a gift from God, and He graciously gifted Richard and Janie with the friendship of Glen and Emily Gravatt, who are generous in their giving and enjoyable to be around. They are easy to be vulnerable and transparent with and share deeper thoughts and doubts with. This is still a relatively new friendship but one rife with possibilities.

A word of caution gleaned from many years of observation and practice: beware becoming friends with your children. A child should not have the burden of being a parent's best friend. Parents should nurture, guide, teach, encourage, and discipline children but not be their confidants. Being a friend and confidant of a child greatly harms both parent and child. Treat your adult children with respect and love. Let them navigate through their own lives, managing their own estates. Love them, enjoy them, and leave them be, free of your fears, doubts, and secret sins, which are things only a dear friend should know.

CHAPTER 20

New Church Home

As life unfolded for the Pattersons, they became very involved with the home group Janie had attended for twenty-plus years and content in attending the church pastored by Dr. Gene Getz. During that time, Joshua was finishing four years of training at Dallas Theological Seminary and had developed a relationship with Matt Chandler, a gifted, charismatic, and dynamic young preacher. This new young church was thriving and rapidly growing. Matt wanted Josh to come on staff and use his gifts of administration to become the executive pastor. At the same time, Richard and Janie felt the Holy Spirit drawing them away from their longtime church home.

Josh came to his dad one day, asking if he would attend Matt's church to check it out, making sure it was not a cult. The next Sunday, when visiting the Village Church, Janie and Richard sensed a powerful presence of the Holy Spirit. As they walked to secure a seat, a tall, lanky man came toward them, leaping over rows of chairs, to greet them. His first words were "You must be Josh's parents." Having never met the man, Richard was taken aback when he said, "I have been flirting with and wooing your son to come on staff to help us." Richard had never met a man who unabashedly and enthusiastically spoke in that manner.

After that brief introduction, Matt started to preach. His passion and anointing were evident; the preaching was nothing they had heard before. Upon leaving, they were spellbound, realizing God had orchestrated everything for that moment. They soon joined the Village Church, starting a journey that continues to this day.

Both served the church body, with Richard eventually being asked by Matt to serve on the elder board, which he did for eight years. The church grew rapidly to about twelve thousand congregants, with elders guiding, praying, and teaching the people. It was a sobering and humbling experience, with Richard learning much about himself. His many sins of pride, arrogance, judgment, and fear of man were exposed to the light. A number of times, Richard was rebuked or corrected in the elder room for some offense. But out of this refining fire emerged a humbler, gentler, and more contrite Richard. In the end, it was all necessary discipline. What a privilege it was to serve with the other men as an elder.

There were many retreats, seminars, and instructions that molded these men. An interesting one involved a yearlong once-a-week teaching on spiritual warfare, taught by a young pastor from Houston who had been born and raised in Africa. He had keen eyesight and understanding concerning this type of warfare. His teaching to Richard and about ten others was fascinating information about demons and the deliverance of such from people. Richard learned that demonic attacks were a real thing, and he was able to participate in a number of deliverances from these demonic forces. In these deliverances, he actually spoke with various demons, ordering them to leave the person they were infesting. The exorcism was not at all like what was depicted in the movies; it was usually quiet and well controlled with God, who was sovereign over all. But it was still unnerving to hear a demon speak; in fact, it could be terrifying. However, Richard learned much during his tenure as an elder.

Another aspect of God's involvement in Richard's sanctification was music. Music had always been important to Richard, even as a young boy. His first real exposure was at age nine, with a school field trip to visit the Los Angeles Philharmonic. He was mesmerized by the sound coming from the orchestra. Shortly thereafter, he started taking piano lessons along with his two sisters. Three different lady teachers taught him the basics. The last teacher was probably Russian and was the best trained of the three. She also introduced Richard to avocados. The fruit was expensive, so it was rarely eaten at home, but at her home, it seemed there was an unlimited quantity to eat. She encouraged Richard to eat all he wanted, and to this day, he still marvels at her kindness in that simple act of giving.

After a few years of lessons, Richard quit, thinking he might become too feminized by continuing the lessons. However, he was still strongly drawn to music, so he found a young man who taught him, at no cost, the wonders of classical music. Throughout his adult life, Richard taught himself new pieces. Of course, he was undisciplined and lazy and kept repeating the same errors instead of correcting them. At that point, Mary Anderson, his last teacher, entered his life.

Richard, who was reluctant to begin lessons again at age fifty-five, was persuaded by Janie to at least meet with this gracious older lady. When he met Mary, she asked him to play something, so he performed a Chopin waltz he had taught himself. Upon his completing the piece, she said it was good, and what did he expect from taking lessons from her? Richard told her he cheated at playing music. He needed help in correcting bad fingering, bad timing, and other mistakes instead of repeating them, as well as instruction in music theory and help to feel the music and not just bang out the notes. She said she could help, and thus began a twenty-year love affair with music and a deep and tender relationship with Mary and husband, Raymond.

Early on, Richard came to know Mary as a mature, well-grounded Christian lady. She and Richard often spent half the time speaking of Jesus and the other half on a lesson. The times spent with Mary and Raymond were instrumental in the maturation of Richard's spiritual life. She also encouraged him to stretch himself by entering piano competitions and playing jazz pieces or recitals of classical music. Of course, this terrified him. Losing sleep over upcoming recitals, Richard finally quit the lessons, but he maintained a close relationship with this godly woman. God put Mary into Richard's life for two obvious reasons: to teach him music and to aid him in his Christian walk of sanctification. To this day, he spends as much time with her as possible. She is undoubtedly the simplest, most righteous person he knows. Richard now composes music and lyrics and immensely enjoys playing the piano. He has learned to continue to play through wrong notes, learning this from Beethoven, who stated, "There are no wrong notes, just music." There is freedom in wrong notes and the silent beauty between them.

CHAPTER 21

Grandchildren

Among the many fascinating things at that time in Richard's life, the outstanding event was the introduction of grandchildren. The union of Natalie and Josh produced four beautiful and exceptional children. All children, of course, are exceptional; this certainly was the case concerning Lily, Luke, Liv, and Lucy. Each of these children was tenderly written about in Richard's first book of poetry: *Cor Meum Poetry: Poetry of My Heart*.

Josh and Natalie eventually married after seven years of dating and courting. Natalie is everything one could hope for in a daughter-in-law. No one is perfect, but she approaches this gold standard. Beautiful and wise, with many being honored to call her a friend, she is the rare one who does not gossip or ever talk badly about people. She is an utter joy to be around, except when playing Monopoly or any other game. She is ruthless and will not budge, bend a rule, or show any mercy. She usually wins, and the good-natured bantering after each game is well received.

Natalie bore Richard's first grandchild, Lily Marie Patterson. What unmitigated joy and wonderment Richard felt upon meeting Lily. She was more than imagined: a pretty, precocious, prancing princess. All the family members lost their minds over this little one. Again, Richard had an overwhelming feeling of sacrificial love and protection for this baby. The love for a grandchild is different from the love one has for his or her own children. It's hard to explain, but most grandparents experience it. The way God has structured people, it is evident that there is a never-ending fount of love pouring from their hearts. Each child, grandchild, sister, brother, mother, father, or friend has access to this bottomless well. It is another mystery of God.

Each subsequent grandchild released the same emotions. Luke Rice Patterson was born about two years later, and to date, he is Richard's only grandson. Scent is a powerful sense, and it appeared baby Luke was drawn to Grandpa's pheromonal emanations and vice versa. They bonded strongly, almost as if conjoined. Now, at twelve years of age, Luke appears to be coming into his own, developing as an amazing young person. He is intelligent and handsome and has a good sense of who and whose he is. He should have a fulfilled and exciting life.

Liv Sophia Patterson, now ten years old, was born next. She is always laughing, even when trying to be mad, and she loves exploring life. Strong-willed, she takes after her uncle Jared in that department. She is gorgeous and outgoing, willing to try new things, always sees the world through different-colored lenses, and is an acute observer, missing little. She would rather have an orange than a cookie.

Next came Lucy Joy Patterson. She is all and in everything a girl. Always in dresses, she exudes femininity. A bright little girl of eight, she captures everyone's heart by being genuinely interested in others. She remembers everything and is tenderhearted and filled with cascades of kisses and love.

God has blessed all four children with physical beauty, high intelligence, and social graces. They are also blessed by having the most exceptional parents one could wish for. Josh and Natalie are raising their children well, preparing them to become healthy adults and good citizens. This is the healthiest family unit Richard has ever witnessed.

Having diapers changed, feeding, and spending days and nights with them, the grandchildren became important fixtures in the lives of Richard and Janie. Year after year, investing in their lives has brought great joy and reward reminiscent of what the psalmist said about grandchildren being like crowns upon one's head. As they grow older, of course, things change—no more diaper changes or sleeping in bed with grandparents when feeling scared. Skinned knees are replaced by homecoming at school and, soon enough, driving lessons for Lily.

Change is inevitable and often bothersome. As Richard ages, the realities of the circle of life are impressed upon him. Janie and Richard hope they will live long enough to see these wonderful grandchildren become adults and witness their lives unfold. These children all love and fear God, walking unabashedly with Him.

CHAPTER 22

Consequences

The counterweight to the wonderful story of grandchildren is the sad struggle of all concerning the aftermath of Richard's divorce. Due to many circumstances too numerous to mention, a toxic milieu developed, with everyone trying in his or her own way to navigate through the maze. Janie's divorce from her unfaithful husband affected little three-year-old Troy, with challenges still manifesting in this fifty-year-old man. The dissolution of Richard's marriage had a profound impact on Jared and Josh.

Josh, upon having an impactful encounter with God at age nineteen, started healing, which resulted in the aforementioned success in marriage and children. Jared's tortuous journey toward healing has been painful. He is a gentle, intelligent, compassionate, nonjudgmental, humble man everyone enjoys being around. He was married after his favorite and only grandmother died, a harbinger shadow of things to come.

Richard's mother, known as Granny, came to live with him and Janie for the last seven years of her life. It was a special time, with all thoroughly enjoying the time spent with her. God, being gracious, gave her ninety-three years of good health, with only the last two weeks spent in the care of hospice in the upstairs room of Richard's home.

As his mom lay in the hospital bed with a jaundiced pallor, she and Richard had a few moments alone. Staring stoically at Richard, she asked, "It's bad, isn't it?"

Richard replied, "Yes, Mom, it's bad; it does not appear you will recover from this." Then he began to quietly cry.

Taking hold of his hand, she tried to comfort him and lessen his bereavement, saying, "Son, you know I can't live forever."

But Richard always had thought she would; she was his forever-young mom, defender of family, a mama bear with her cubs. Now she was only two weeks away from her final rest, laying her beautiful head on her pillow of death. When she departed, she passed the baton to Richard, Shirley, and Suzie; Richard was now the reluctant patriarch. What was to be his final legacy?

Family from all parts of the country sat at her bedside, singing hymns, loving her, and reminiscing with her right to the end, when Suzie said, "I think she is gone now."

A hard pivot had to be made the next day as all celebrated Jared's wedding. An old thing dies, and a new thing begins. It was much like when Janie's mom, Helen, died one day, and the next day, Lily was born—again, the circle of life.

However, less than three years later, Jared's marriage came to an end, adding more to Jared's pain. But this story has a happy ending. Because of Jared's hard work at honestly looking at himself, the reward has been a new beginning for him. The disappointments for Jared were manifold, but he learned that the past cannot be changed or wished away. Instead of trying to change the past narrative, which is impossible, it is best to learn from it and begin a new narrative, using one's strengths and gifts. This requires much painful work, but the result is a much more fulfilled life. He is a fighter and a survivor with much wisdom; this bodes well for him. Stumbles and failures are inevitable, but they will be overcome. Possibilities of a new life, a healthy wife, and even a family for himself now exist. Jared is a strong man easy to love, and Richard is his biggest fan, believing all things are possible for him.

Troy's story is somewhat different from but in many ways similar to Jared's. He was married to Cathi for about nineteen years. Everyone loved Cathi, but she and Troy were somewhat enigmatic and secretive. No one really knew what was going on in their lives. All accepted what was offered, but a certain mysteriousness remained. Richard and Cathi had a good relationship; he admired her intelligence and work ethic. Tragically, she developed cervical cancer, which eventually claimed her life at forty-six years of age. She wanted to die at Richard and Janie's home, which she did. She did so upstairs where Granny had passed under hospice care just a year before. Her passing was sudden and unexpected, with only Troy, Janie, and Richard in attendance.

It took Troy a while to regain his footing, but with the help of godly men, Troy's life was ransomed by Christ, and he is a new man. New beginnings are in store for Troy and Jared. The hardships and suffering hopefully are behind them.

There are unrequited things in everyone's life. We all have things we wish we had done or not done and said or not said. Anyone who says he would not change a thing that went before him is probably a fool. We all could do better if given another chance. This is one reason we do a better job with our grandchildren than with our own children. Each day gives us an opportunity to do it over. Nothing can be done about the past. Today is the youngest you will ever be, so work on today to build your legacy and finish your race strong with the accolade of "Well done, my good and faithful servant."

CHAPTER 23

---~m~---

Retirement

When Richard retired from private practice and sold his practice to a young doctor, no real plans were in place for his future. This turned out to be a good thing. He and Janie packed some belongings into his Ford F-150 pickup and took off on a three-week junket. Having no reservations, they traveled to Wyoming, South Dakota, Iowa, Missouri, and other states before returning home, which now was with Karen and Dick McFarland.

Richard had not been retired for more than two months, when he received a call from a friend asking if he might come work with them, as one of their senior doctors was having surgery on his neck. Richard went back to work, helping in a busy practice, until the doctor recovered. This lasted about nine months, giving the practice time to hire a younger doctor and start grooming him to become a partner.

Richard again retired, but he was contacted by an old friend in Baytown, Texas, who needed help in a busy practice he was trying to sell. Janie and Richard traveled to visit with the doctor and his wife and were warmly received. Richard told his friend he would give him an answer on Monday, which was going to be a yes to his generous offer. Before Richard could call the Baytown doctor, however, he received a frantic phone call at eight in the morning from the senior member of the practice he had just helped out six weeks before. The associate who had just had neck surgery had made a decision to end his life. He had shot himself. The remaining senior doctor asked Richard if he could come to the office right away.

When Richard arrived at the office, there was an air of profound sadness and confusion. The deceased, who had been charismatic, successful, handsome, and loved by all, had decided for unknown reasons to end his life. His marriage had been good, his son had just graduated from Vanderbilt University, and his daughter had just arrived home from her honeymoon, with the entire family sharing and enjoying the wedding photos on that Sunday. He appeared to have planned his departure, as all affairs were put in order. No one saw it coming, and it was devastating. Even his best friend of thirty years, who spent every Thursday night in a hot tub with him, sharing a glass of wine and talking about life and its challenges, was completely caught off guard. Evidently, this doctor was not completely known even by his best friend of thirty years.

Richard has been around people who have committed or attempted suicide, including pastors, strong Christians, weak Christians, friends, and acquaintances, and each time, he was shocked. It is difficult to be fully known by anyone, but it is something we should strive for. Who knows when someone might spiral down the black hole of depression or hopelessness? The Enemy is ever ready to whisper into our ears his lies.

Richard worked about a year and a half before the practice regained its footing. Alas, the retirement again was short-lived. Out of the blue, Richard was offered a position at John Peter Smith Hospital, a level-one trauma center in Fort Worth, Texas. The job involved teaching and training fifth- and sixth-year double-degreed residents and first-year interns. The new opportunity was out of

Richard's wheelhouse, as he had always been in private practice and would now be thrust into a teaching environment. Asked to submit a curriculum vitae and specialty board certification, he was offered an interview with the program chairman, Dr. John Stella. Never having met him and knowing little about him, Richard sat in his office, awaiting the interview. Upon his entering, an unusual conversation ensued.

"Hello. I'm Dr. Stella, and you must be Dr. Patterson. I perceive you are a Christian, as I am, and I would like to ask you a few questions. Can you share the gospel of Jesus Christ verbally, and can you place yourself beneath all you encounter at the hospital?"

Richard was stunned at the beautiful boldness and answered yes to both questions. Two hours of questioning later, he was offered the faculty position.

Richard was again surprised and asked why he was offered the position, since he felt he had little to offer in an academic setting. He was assured that an excellent choice had been made and was welcomed to the oral and maxillofacial surgery staff.

That was thirteen years ago. Richard now has many more responsibilities, including clinic director, overseer of the intravenous-sedation clinic, and attending staff in the operating room, supervising residents. But the thing he enjoys most is sharing his faith with everyone, Buddhists, atheists, humanists, Mormons, Muslims, Catholics, strong Christians, weak Christians, Hindus, and all. The door to his office is always open to anyone who might require prayer or just someone to listen to.

Retirement seems to be ever evolving. At seventy-five years of age, Richard is now working only one day per week, which is wonderful. The chairman does not want him to retire and has been gracious in allowing him to map out this journey.

All things come to an end, and this certainly is the case as Richard decides to slow down. There are many emotions at work in the making of this decision. A majority of Richard's life has been spent in the preparation of becoming a doctor and the decades of actually being one. The affirmations by peers, colleagues, and patients will be missed, and the joy of teaching and mentoring will come to an end; fifty-seven years of his life will be set aside.

This will be a difficult transition but one he will surely navigate. Spending time with Janie, their children and grandchildren, and friends; writing; enjoying music; enjoying nature; having coffee with Janie and a spirited drink in the evenings; reading; and watching something on television will fill the days.

CHAPTER 24

———✺———

Final Thoughts

During Richard's semiretirement years, many epiphanies and surprises have occurred. As we age, of course, medical issues begin to present themselves; time and telomeres always win. Richard has been blessed with good health, but the infirmities of age make themselves known. He does not have the stamina, strength, or desire to do the things he did as a younger man. There is a natural slowing down, a pace allowing wonderment and contentment to flourish. Hopefully, introspection occurs, a time for reflection.

How valuable are the gems of friendship, a place of knowing and being known; the strengthening love binding siblings; and a better understanding of the things that are important. Unfortunately, a number of friends and relatives have developed dementia. This slow waltz of decline is difficult to witness. Three of these people have served their country in the military. John Grettenberg was a paratrooper with the 101st Airborne Division, serving from 1959 to 1963. He was deathly afraid of heights, which added to his fear of jumping from an airplane. On most jumps, he vomited, passed out, and revived before landing. It was quite a feat, but he served honorably. John Alvarado served in Vietnam as a marine. Now these two are being robbed of their minds, which is sorrowful to witness. The third, brother-in-law Buddy Helms, served in the navy, on the aircraft carrier *Kearsarge*, from 1958 to 1962 and was also discharged honorably.

Richard has two dear friends suffering from cognitive decline, a friend of forty-three years and another of forty-six years. One has traveled far down this path of no return; all that remains of him are memories. Richard penned a poem about dementia, a terribly sad disease. With more time on hand, Richard and Janie are better able to interact with them.

Being gracious, God is easing Richard and Janie into their elder years. Recognizing the immense importance of family is paramount. With all the drama, warts, and blemishes, we remain connected. The richness of a few dear friends; his undying love for his children and grandchildren; and his ever-deepening, crazy love for Janie will sustain Richard until angels escort him home.

The last word remains with God. Glory and praise abound to Him.

Looking back, Richard reflects on the lives of his parents, Irene and Bill, with amazement and satisfaction. They produced and nurtured three good kids. Both had horrid beginnings and were poorly educated, but they had determination and steadfastness about them. Mother was more focused than Dad, with an incredible iron will concerning what was best for her children. Dad was more malleable and often reluctant in his duties, but he went to work every day, providing for his family. Never a womanizer, drunkard, or scoundrel, he provided for his family. He was just a common man, but he was one of the most intelligent people Richard ever knew. Even though Richard cannot recall his father ever telling him he loved him, Richard knows he did. There was no need for a deep psychological dive to try to figure all this out. It was just Dad being himself, a compilation of his hard life. Richard and his sisters turned out just fine. Mom was totally sacrificial in her dealings with her family, a saintly, unselfish mother.

———\m~———

Most of us have about a forty- or seventy-year run on this earth, with all of us falling far short of perfection. I am in many ways more imperfect than my parents, making mistake after mistake in raising my boys, but I truly believe I did the best I could at the time. My grandchildren are blossoming into marvelous people; this could be our finest legacy. I am told great-grandpa Franklin Lindsey Patterson prayed for his future generations while circuit-riding his horse to rural churches in Arkansas more than 130 years ago.

Thank you for reading this story. I hope you enjoyed it as much as I enjoyed sharing it. Someone once said, "It is an unusual man who has a well-tended grave." Here is hoping that in one or two generations, I will be remembered as having passed through.

Dennis's War Notes

Flanders fields and poppies it's not,
but Vietnam jungle, with its stink and rot.
The Great War a stupid war, the jungle war very same score.
Forgetting Augustine's justified wars,
the diplomats and generals walk right through that door.
It's the blood of the boys that will water these fields,
the maimed and the dying just where they kneel.
Let's posture and bicker about who sits where
while another unknown son dies on an unnamed hill.
No tree of liberty watered by their precious blood,
this nothing more than a vile crimson flood.
You old men come have your look;
tour the headstones listed in the tourist books.
Dennis, my friend I loved so well, died
in the jungle just where he fell.
He could not care less or pronounce the name
of that foreign village that staked its death claim.
His and his brothers' blood drenched the ground;
we back home never heard a sound.
Their sacrifice on our soft behalf, hometown flags flying half-mast.
We must fight our wars if we are attacked; all
other conflicts we should just stand pat.
Our boys' blood too precious to spill at
unnamed villages and unknown hills.
I am sure Dennis would rather have been in his mother's
arms, she singing a lullaby until breaking dawn.

We should review what Augustine had to say; war
should be limited and proceed in this way.
I want our boys to grow up strong and not have their
bodies littering fields where they don't belong.
If they must die, let them die here defending
our liberty, our freedoms so dear.

Soldier's Lament

I shall meet my end in death,
will take my life, blood, and breath.
Resting in a dreamless sleep,
God ordained me to the deep.
Closing of eye, quenching of breath, a
soldier's tryst, a loveless death.
Standing he upon native land
would rather not wander foreign strand.
With truth and reason on his side, he
goes to battle, turmoil inside.
Our glorious nation, its heroes bestride
known, unknown, sung, unsung, stepping side by side.

Foes flung like foreign dung,
our precious boys sundered, undone.
Every desert, field, and shore,
their bodies' monuments a ghastly score.
From Concord to Gettysburg, Flanders to Hamburg,
Bastogne to Rome, ice of chosen
marines frigid, frozen.
Inchon to Mekong,
our boys' sabers blood have drawn.
Pelelieu to Saipan too,
brothers fall, bidding us fair adieu.
Restless, going to and fro, finger of death from sky aglow.
Some will fall; there they lie.
Will they be remembered as they die?
Oh, go quickly; quickly go. You died bravely; this we know!

The battle hell you knew well—booming cannon, shrieking shell.
With bursting heart, an oath on high we
swear, you are always by our side,
with battle blood so gory adorning your robes of glory.
The grass on graves quiver, these eidolons make one shiver.
Awaiting Judgment Day,
the ashen and the gray.
Soft voices calling
to ones who are falling.
Mourning dove cooing,
its plaintive sound wooing.
As Ezekiel prophesied dry bones to life,
receiving a crown at last trumpet sound.
On this eternal hallowed ground,
cherubim station guards around.
Rest, all you our sainted dead; no more will death on you tread.
Your fame and valor you will keep
in your blissful, dreamless sleep.
We will in song and story tell every detail of how you fell,
wrap you in a tearful shroud
in reverence as our heads are bowed.

1917

The grip is tightening still of woe upon the land,
  bitter black trouble seeping into the sand.
These boys so beautiful, all being so brave, pulled
  from trenches and pushed into their graves.
Baby boys so early from suckling upon the breast,
  young men now shuffling to their eternal rest.

The rainbow tears of mothers, heart filled with fear, no
  reprieve from anguish by shedding of those tears.
The hope of a father, these boys becoming men,
  his tortured heart twisted, knowing this is their end.
You, my son, will have no son: the bitterness I weep,
  beautiful son; my lovely son now goes into the deep.
In other lands, under stranger sod, foreign feet now softly trod,
  not knowing this my baby boy on my breast would nod.
Weary hearts have grown with sorrows and our moans as
  these boys in your fields were scattered and were sown.
I don't sleep well at night; the wind seems bitter cold,
  but I dream oft of my son. He was brave and bold.

Friendship

A mighty mountain rising from a plain is a
person, *friend* moniker for a name.
Some linger a lengthy bit, others gone in a hop and a skip.
Each serving a special need,
a stanchion, a pillar, a wavering reed.
This one I would die for but now can get lost,
my needs so fickle and come at great cost.
I am fair-weathered, and so are they;
many file through, but few will stay.
You must know me inside and out,
my shine, my stain, my sin, my pout.
If you don't turn and depart from me, if
you don't faint from all you see,
then I might gaze and discern upon you,
judging you harshly to see what you do.
If you are still standing with love in your heart,
a friendship beginning a glorious start.
You seem to know me, all pretenses being gone.
I am just myself; for this, I have longed.
Know, being known, no averting of eye,
you love me with all my warts and my sty.
This happens rarely, a few times in one's life, all
others just fillers where drama is rife.
This one I know, and they know me,
speaking or silence, whatever we please.
Near or distant matters little to us; boundaries
and spatials just a mere fuss.

Time goes by; the relationship grows,
souls reverberating, resonating love shows.
This good gift of God a foretaste of glory—no
shielding or veil, just my blemished story.
I am as you see me: needy and weak.
These saints, these friends, the ones that I seek.

Friend

Walk a mile with me, friend,
entering my life in a casual way, holding forth and
chatting gay. Others came, deciding not to stay.
You, my friend, stayed and played.
Passersby not one heeded.
You, my friend, sensed what I needed. Dear
you, fashioning dreams of heart,
you, friend, did your part. Holding forth 'neath
heaven or hell, shall never bid you farewell.

Two Brothers

Never having had a brother, two sisters would suffice;
having had a brother, I think, would have been nice.
Two sons I sired; brothers they would be.
Normal competition is what all would see.
First being older by three years, it's true;
little brother two loved him through and through.
As years followed days, the first went his own way,
leaving little brother to manage his own play.
Younger brothers often see what older brothers do,
the good, the bad, the ugly, lessons he will rue.
Older being directed by the wisdom of this world,
younger one struggling, around he would swirl.
No time for each other put distance twixt the two,
growing and drifting, not knowing what to do.
The boys loved each other, paralyzed in their fears,
growing further apart, would never be close or near.
Time being the healer, change on the way,
blood thicker than water, I believe is what they say.
Growing older day by day with love in their hearts,
let's go back to the beginning and get a new start.
Reconciliation; the Son paves the way,
renewal of their hearts, new hope for the day.

Blended

Two marriages coming to an end—
in spite of coaxing, the arc would not bend.
Parents just chasing the wind.
The man left with two sons, the woman with her one.
No one wins when it's all said and done.
Everyone suffers as the dark forces gloat, demons, devils cheering,
as they sink this sacred boat.
None anchored by scriptures in the countervailing gale,
mother, father, children falling off the rails.
Struggling many years,
acting as father and mother,
it's so much better being one or the other.
The single mother rolling up her sleeves, raising her only son,
when it's all said and done.
Single father, with tremendous toil, tries his very best
for his two little boys.

Deep scars are etched in everybody's soul;
all concerned pay a very heavy toll.
Mistake after mistake piles up in their
lives, taking every wrong turn,
chasing every lie.
But God, in His mercy,
started healing this rent;
the Matchmaker in heaven a new marriage sent.

He blended two families, and the healing
begins: three brothers, two parents,
arc starting to bend.
This marriage will last lessons learned from the past.
God, being the cynosure, holds this new family fast.

ABOUT THE AUTHOR

Dr. Richard Patterson developed a passion for writing late in life. He has two published books of poetry, *Cor Meum Poetry* and *Cor Meum Redux*. He has always enjoyed music, especially the great classical and romantic composers, and takes great pleasure in playing many of their pieces on the piano. He composes music often in the hymnal format or in the genre of relaxing melodies. Richard is married to his beloved best friend, Janie, who inspires him. He has three sons and four marvelous grandchildren, who are his true delight.

At seventy-six years of age, Dr. Patterson still works part-time in the training of interns and residents in the specialty of oral maxillofacial surgery. Whether it's coffee in the morning with Janie or dinner with dear friends, time seems to have tempered, allowing him contentment and wonderment.

Printed in the United States
by Baker & Taylor Publisher Services